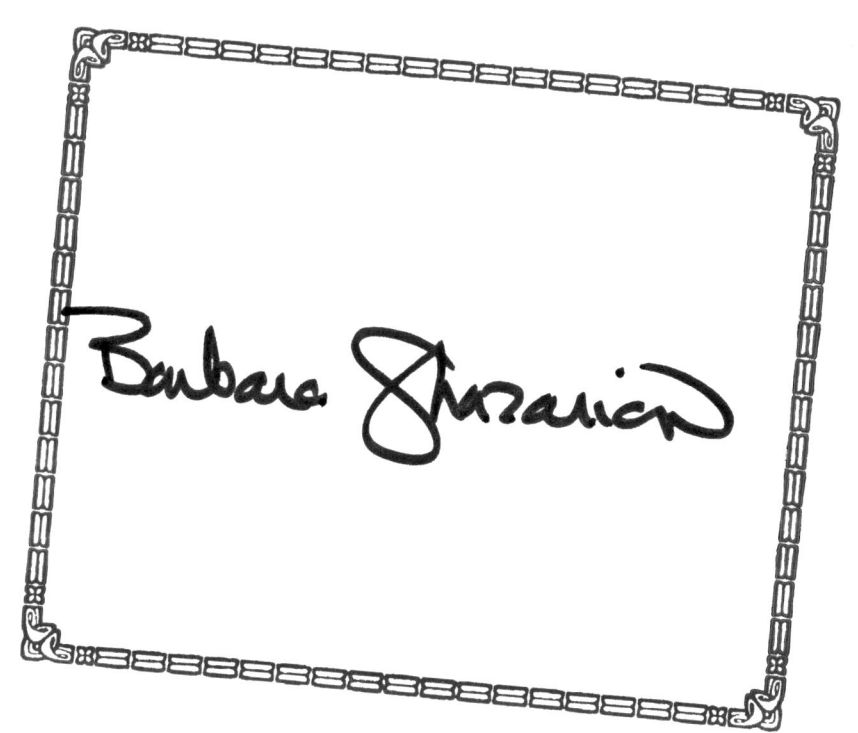

DESCENDANTS OF NOAH
Christian Stories from the Armenian Heart

Descendants of Noah

Christian Stories from the Armenian Heart

Compiled and Edited by
Barbara Ghazarian

Second Edition
Mayreni Publishing
2005

Also by **Barbara Ghazarian**

Simply Armenian: Naturally Healthy Ethnic Cooking Made Easy

ISBN: 1-931834-08-3
ISBN: 978-1-931834-04-9

Library of Congress Control Number: 2002113089

Ghazarian, Barbara
  Descendants of Noah: Christian Stories from the Armenian Heart
    Formerly published under the title of *Descendants of Noah: Stories of Armenian Faith and Heritage*

1. Religion, Christianity, Orthodox, Armenian.
2. Inspiration, Christian, Armenian.

Printed in the United States
Printings: 02-1, 05-2

Copyright © 2002 by Barbara Ghazarian
All rights reserved. No part of this publication may be reproduced or transmitted in any form or by any means, electronic or mechanical, including any information storage retrieval system, without written permission from the publisher.

Mayreni Publishing
P.O. Box 5881
Monterey, CA 93944, U.S.A.
http://mayreni.com

Special bulk-rate discounts are available on this and other Mayreni Publishing books. Companies and organizations may purchase books for premiums or resale by contacting Mayreni Publishing at the above address.

MAYRENI PUBLISHING, 2002, 2005

Foreword

For nearly two millennia, the Armenian people have turned to the Bible for inspiration and spiritual guidance. Their resilience and dedication to God has survived countless invasions, continuous persecution, massacres, and genocide.

According to scripture, after the great flood, Noah's Ark came to rest atop Mt. Ararat, the highest point in historic Armenia. Nestled in the Caucasus Mountains and the Anatolian Peninsula (in what is at times referred to as the "cradle of civilization"), Armenians have long prided themselves as being descendants of Noah.

In 301 A.D, Armenians took an unprecedented leap of faith by adopting Christianity as their state religion, and Armenia became a testing ground for that faith. It was destined to be conquered by more powerful and hostile neighbors as well as invaders from the East.

Romans, Parthians, Byzantines, Mongols, Arabs, and Turks all attempted to impose their will upon the Armenian people. Yet the Armenians never renounced their beliefs or their faith. Instead, these invasions and massacres strengthened the Armenian resolve.

In 1915, with most of historic Armenia under the rule of the crumbling Ottoman Turkish Empire, Armenians, along with other Christian minorities, were persecuted. Turkic nationalism and the religious fanaticism that took hold of their overlords resulted in the first genocide of the 20th century. More than 1.5 million Armenian men, women, and children were martyred. Genocide tested the faith of the Armenian people again. Despite a national dispersion into a global Diaspora, the Armenian nation survived.

What little remained of the historic Armenian lands were absorbed into the Soviet Empire soon after, and, for nearly seventy years, Armenian Christianity was attacked by the atheist ideals of the Communist regimes. But once again, the church and the people's faith survived.

In September 2001, as the eyes of the world focused on the terrorist attacks in New York City and Washington, D.C., Armenia quietly and fittingly celebrated its tenth anniversary of independence from Soviet rule and its 1700th anniversary as a Christian nation. Pope John Paul II made a pilgrimage to Armenia to stand witness to this tiny nation's dedication to

Christ through centuries of oppression. For the whole world and for all the children of God who were coping with the shock and loss of September 11, the Pope drew inspiration from the Armenian example of faith and survival.

Armenians know the pain of loss and injustice, yet through it all they have continued to find salvation in the Bible, known in Armenian as *Asdvadzashoonch* (the Breath of God). Highlighted by prayer and practice, the history of Armenian Christianity—and even Armenia—has been a story of endurance, sacrifice, salvation, and hope.

Each Armenian carries a story that embodies these beliefs and this history in some way. *Descendants of Noah: Christian Stories from the Armenian Heart* is a collection of true stories about, and recollections by, Armenian Americans connected to the Armenian Apostolic Church in the United States. Each story highlights a moment or an event or an aspect of the spiritual journey when Armenian faith or heritage helped lift the person above the malaise and chaos of a world that is at times overwhelming and always shifting.

In these trying times, Armenian Americans continue to pray and worship, knowing that the spiritual journey and the testing of one's faith is a continuous process. The power of their collective story bears witness not only to Armenians' tenacity to survive but also to the resiliency of their Christian beliefs. Let this book serve as a beacon of hope and a source of inspiration for all Armenians, for us as Americans, and to the world as well.

Ardashes Kassakhian
Glendale, California

Introduction to the Second Edition

Who are the Armenians?

The Armenian nation, where East meets West, is the oldest Christian nation in the world. The Armenian Apostolic Orthodox Church traces its succession from Christ's disciples, Saints Thaddaeus and Bartholomew, who preached and were martyred in Armenia. By 301 A.D., Christianity was proclaimed the official state religion, replacing almost one thousand years of Zoroastrianism. They have never turned back.

If you are not Armenian, why explore faith within the context of the Armenian Christian experience?

Because the Armenian story is continuous testimony in modern times that Jesus Christ's life and resurrection are a moving force in the world.

What can you learn from them?

The power of Christ's resilience. The value of tolerance. Armenian Christians are known throughout the world for their tolerance towards other churches and other systems of thought and doctrine.

For most of their history, the Armenians have lived with and among others in harmony.

Tragically, war and unrest often bring trials and tests. The Armenians were massacred almost to extinction in the 1915 Genocide. Yet, they endured, and in 1991, upon the breakup of the Soviet Union, the Armenian nation resurrected itself once again as an independent country. Today, this remnant of historic Armenia measures the size of New Jersey and is sandwiched between Iran, Turkey, Georgia, and Azerbaijan.

In a world still abounding with religious intolerance, persecutions, and genocides, the Armenians have always had a choice and they have always chosen Christ—even when threatened by extermination. Yet, the story of the Armenian people's enduring faith remains largely untold.

Motivated by a personal belief that faith is experiential and best shared by example, I thought it was time to share the Armenian Christian experience with others. And what better way to communicate "living faith" across cultures than through stories?

The idea of soliciting ministry from a wide variety of people in the greater Armenian-American community intrigued Reverend Father Dajad

Davidian, a long-time pastor of one of the largest Armenian Apostolic parishes in the United States. Together, we developed two sets of questions, one exploring different aspects of faith, and the other focusing on the role of the Armenian Christian heritage in people's lives.

More than ninety people shared hundreds of personal experiences of faith and heritage with me in phone interviews. Over one-third of their testimonies, each highlighting a moment or an event or an aspect of the spiritual journey when Armenian faith or heritage uplifted the spirit, were first published in 2002 as *Descendants of Noah: Stories of Armenian Apostolic Faith and Heritage*.

In the years since, I've shared these stories with many people across the country and come to realize that *Descendants of Noah* has a story for every person and occasion. Regardless of nationality, ethnic heritage, or religious tradition, people seeking comfort and a deeper understanding of their spirituality have found themselves, and the stories of their own journeys, reflected in the experiences shared by the storytellers who opened their hearts and lives in this collection. Those practicing daily devotions or taking part in Bible study groups sight the Armenian's unique perspective as enriching their own.

As with the story of Noah and countless others throughout the Bible to Christ and his disciples, the voices in *Descendants of Noah* tell a story of faith, tenacity, and resilience.

At any point, the critical mass of Armenians could have concluded that Christianity wasn't making a lot of sense. *Descendants of Noah* proves that Jesus Christ lives today in the hearts and souls of these ancient Christians and that the Armenian Church remains a keystone of the Armenian culture.

I believe that witnessing someone else's faith can be a powerful and lasting experience. I hope that witnessing this tiny Christian nation's resilience will, at the very least, flood your heart with awe-inspired respect.

For this second edition, all contributor's names and stories are listed in the Index of Storytellers. A Thematic Index has been added to make it easier to find stories by topic, and I have included the original interview questions and response readings as a Study and Workshop Guide.

Barbara Ghazarian
Compiler and Editor

Primate's Word

"Christ is revealed among us! No other words carry so much hope and meaning for human life. The feeling seems especially powerful during the Easter season, as we remember the events surrounding Christ's resurrection. Just imagine what it was like to be among the disciples on the day when our Risen Lord appeared before them. In that instant, it must have seemed like the entire world had changed. And in the truest sense, it had!

"And yet, we do not have to 'just imagine' what it was like. As members of the Holy Apostolic Church—the institution established by Christ Himself—we can actually experience that world-changing moment. We can enter into the real presence of the living, resurrected Christ. And we can do so every week, every time we participate in the holy *badarak*."

Excerpt from the 2002 Easter message of Archbishop Khajag Barsamian, Primate of the Diocese of the Armenian Church of America (Eastern)

Contents

FAITH
My Life's Motto	17
The Spokesman	19
A Headache	21
Living in Soul	22
Haroutiun: The Resurrection	24
Alzheimer's and the Gift of Love	25
A Small Kindness Reaps Big Rewards	26
It's Never Too Late to Accept God	27
Life-or-Death Decisions	29
Snow Is My Sign from God	32
Snowflakes	34
Holding the Little Cross	34
Prodigal Son	35
Paul's Back	36
The Devil in One Ear and the Angel in the Other	38
Getting Out of the Way	38
Don't Cry, Son	39
Fear of Death	39
I Want to Go Now, Mary	40
Cancer: A Story from Four Perspectives	41
A Road Less Traveled	44
Smile That Smile	47
An Old Georgian Woman	48
Pass It Forward	50
The Almond Seed	51
Tiny Increments of Hope and Progress	52
You Go On	53
Turn to God with Hope	53
Balaam's Donkey	54
A Lesson in Patience	55
Keeping Honest	56
Growing into Iconographic Art	57

Healing Dreams	58
In the Footsteps of Job	59
Traffic Jam	60
The Invisible Hand of the Lord	61
A Tribute to the Memory of the Simsarians	62
When I Lost My Mom I Lost My Faith	63
Answered Prayers	65
The Hand of God	66
A Personal Experience with Angels	67
Defying the Odds	69
The Power of Prayer	70
Nowhere to Take Her	72
Life Choices	73
A Holy Thursday Healing	74
Focal Points of Peace	75
Regular Maintenance	75
Francine	76
Do You Believe in God?	78
The Potato Crop	79
I Wept	80
Pride	81
My First Job in Forty-Three Years	83
A Long Struggle with Divorce	84
Talking to God	85
No Guarantees	86

HERITAGE

A Piece of the Puzzle	91
Witness	93
Conversion Was an Option	93
Bringing the Flame of St. Gregory to Cleveland	94
An Armenian Picnic in Seattle	98
Wanderings	99
The Church in Yettem	101
My Father Loved Cowboy Movies	101
The Kid Who Did Not Become a Priest in Jerusalem	102
A Special Baptism	104
Church Unity	105
Working for Armenia	107

Birth of a Parish	108
Sacrifice	112
The Story of a Mission Parish	113
The Question of Survival	115
Understanding the Liturgy	116
Learning About the Faith from My Children	118
I Go to Church for Me	119
Problems with the Priest	119
Prepared to Lead	120
Throw It Up to the Lord	121
Who Is Armenian?	123
Respecting the Diversity Among Us	125
Reverse Assimilation	126
Cultural Background Makes a Difference	127
Stuffed Vegetables	128
Sunday Drives	128
Rank and File	129
Silent Service and Support	129
My Little Angel	130
The Art of Incensing	132
A Sunday School Christmas Project	132
My Photographs	133
Serving Through the Kitchen	134
A Behind-the-Scenes Look at a Funeral *Hokejash*	135
Taking the Church to Them	136
Participating in the Holiday Folk Fair	137
The Lesson of the Good Samaritan	138
A Little Girl's Service	139
The Messenger	140
Being There for People Is Part of the Job	144
A Tax Collector's Perspective	145
Who Gives What	145
An Odd Rule	146
No Limelight for Me	147
The Armenian Church's Place in the World	148
The Encyclopedia of Religion	150
The Gathering of Christians	151
Our World Reputation	152
Go Back to the Church of Your Ancestors	153

Vow of Silence	155
No Longer Pinching Myself	156
The Lesson of the Prodigal Son	159
Divided We Fall	160
A Matter of Comfort	161
Everything Worthwhile Takes Effort	161
Tradition Smiled on Me	162
Old Book of Prayers	163
Good Turk, Bad Turk	164
Open Your Eyes to the Truth	165
April 24	166
Becoming Adults	166
The Armenian-American Paradox	167
Insights on a College Date	168
STUDY AND WORKSHOP GUIDE	169
THEMATIC INDEX	172
INDEX OF STORYTELLERS	174

Faith

My Life's Motto

I grew up in Beirut, the oldest of three sisters in my family. Our house was a forty-five-minute walk from the closest Armenian Church. On Sunday mornings, my mother had to stay home with the younger children, so she sent me alone to Sunday School. I was required to recount that morning's lesson to my mother and sisters when I returned home. In order not to forget what the Sunday School teacher had said that day, I would repeat the lesson story over and over again while walking home through the streets of Beirut.

One Sunday the story was about a pharmacist and his best friend. The two friends agreed in everything except religion. The pharmacist did not believe in God. His best friend did. One day the pharmacist's best friend had to move to another city. Before he left he took his friend aside and said, "I know you don't believe in God, but, if you find yourself in trouble, promise me that you will fall to your knees and ask for His help. I know He will help you." The pharmacist laughed and bid his friend good-bye.

In the village where the pharmacist had his shop lived a widow who washed clothes for a living. She worked hard and was very poor. One day she fell sick. The neighbors collected enough money to pay for a doctor to visit her. He prescribed some medicine. He instructed the woman's young daughter to take the prescription to the pharmacy that our pharmacist owned and to return as quickly as possible, or her mother might die.

The little girl did as she was told, but, as the pharmacist was putting away the ingredients he had mixed together for her mother, he discovered that he had mixed the wrong ingredients together and the potion he had given the little girl would kill the patient.

Panicked, he raced out of the store and searched the nearby streets for the little girl. He looked everywhere for her. He asked everybody. No one had seen her. Exhausted and very upset, he walked back to the store. As he was walking he remembered his best friend's parting words. He didn't believe, but he was desperate. So at the back of the store near the sofa where he laid down at noon, he lowered himself to his knees and said, "God, please show me you exist and help me."

As he was praying, there was a knock on the door. The police are here to take me away, he thought, but when he opened the door he found the little girl standing there, crying. In her hurry to take the medicine home, she had fallen down, broken the bottle, and injured her hand. She begged the pharmacist to replace the medicine, knowing that she did not have the money to pay for it.

The pharmacist was more than a little relieved to see the girl and to hear how she had spilled the wrongly mixed potion. He attended to her hand, mixed the proper medication, and sent the girl home, knowing that God had answered his prayers and come to his rescue.

The Sunday School teacher who told me the story that morning had said the lesson of the story was that, if you ask for God's help, He will help you. But as I repeated the story to myself on my long walk home from church that day, I began to ask myself how would I have felt and what would I have done if I had been that little girl?

If I had been the one to fall and spill my mother's precious medicine, I would have been very upset with God. Already I would have been angry that my father had died, but, on top of that pain, because I fell and broke the medicine bottle, my mother might die too. In addition, I thought how unfair it would seem that I had hurt my hand, and to make matters worse I would then be faced with having to beg the pharmacist to replace the medication for free.

Putting myself into the little girl's shoes made me realize that she did not know the whole story. She had no idea that she was being used as a tool to bring the pharmacist into faith. It suddenly hit me how in every bad thing that happens from my perspective, there may be a hidden good that has also happened which I may never realize or see. That understanding became the motto of my life. When bad things happen to me, and I begin to complain to God, I stop and I remind myself of the lesson I learned that day—In every bad happening there is something good hidden.

Cecil Keshishian, *Los Angeles, California*

THE SPOKESMAN

I grew up in a traditional Armenian family. My parents went to church every Sunday, and I tagged along as most Armenian kids do. I went to school, got my education, started a business, and became successful in many ways. I was successful financially. I held leadership positions in a few of the local Armenian organizations. I lived in a nice house with a wonderful family.

Everything was going along well until the early 1990s when my company hit a wall. In 1993, the economy in my industry collapsed. I began to experience severe financial problems. Soon, my whole world came crashing down around me. I was on the edge of losing everything I valued and had worked for. Had I gone over the edge, today I would be at Star Market bagging groceries. I came that close to being totally wiped out. My kids would have had to leave school. My wife would have had to work at whatever job she could find. We would have lost our home.

At my darkest moment, when I did not know where to turn, I realized that the only person who could help me was God, with His divine grace. I was a churchgoer before my crisis, but in hindsight it seems I may have been just going though the motions. On the brink of losing everything, I recommitted myself to God and to truly believing in Jesus Christ. I began praying regularly, taking communion every Sunday, reading the Bible on my own, and getting more involved in church, including teaching Sunday School.

The last nine years have been hell on earth as far as business is concerned, but now I think that what I went through, and what I am still going through, has been a blessing for me and for my family. My crisis made me realize that everything was not going to be given to me on a silver platter. In my mind it was God saying to me, "Don't forget who's the boss."

I got a wake-up call. When it seemed like the whole world was collapsing on me, I realized there were many wonderful things in my world that I had ignored.

My family and community were there supporting me. Not once did my wife complain. It was a good lesson for my kids, too. You know how some kids are born with parents who have made it and they grow up assuming that they are entitled to the best. Before my financial problems, my kids may have been like those kids, but I've had to tell them the truth—that they are not going to get anything from me—that they are going to have to go out into the world and make the most of their own lives. Although it was hard to face, I think it was one of the good things that came out of my problems. And when I think about all the people who offered to help me when I was down and out, I get very emotional. Friends gave me significant amounts of money without asking me how or when or if I would repay them. The community rallied. They had faith in me.

I'm more religious than I was before, and I've become a spokesman. The past few years I've been teaching sixth grade Sunday School. I'm not sure I would be teaching Sunday School if I had not gone through what I did. I tell the kids my story—what Haig Deranian went through. Not someone out of the Bible, but someone who is alive today. I tell them that I survived because of my faith in God and because of His divine grace. I use myself as an example that, if they believe in something and if they work hard, then they can attain their dreams.

Today my company is moving in the right direction, and my life is back to normal. When people have problems, I talk to them and tell them my story. God gave me a second chance. I'm grateful and I don't take anything for granted anymore.

Haig Deranian, *Belmont, Massachusetts*

A Headache

The first few days at seminary, I returned to my room after my Old Testament class with a huge headache. I lay on my bed just staring at the ceiling, thinking, how could this be? In class, we had begun to learn about the Bible from a critical perspective rather than from a spiritual one. We were learning about the people who wrote it and the methods used throughout the ages to pass the Gospel down to us. I was discovering a human element that I had not been aware of before. I learned how scribes copying the text did not just copy it, but made decisions to phrase things one way or another that could change the meaning from the original. I discovered that the Prophet Isaiah did not write the whole book of Isaiah. Someone else wrote parts of it.

Until then I had thought the Bible was perfect. Suddenly, there were all these questions. My head hurt because what I had thought was perfect now seemed like one big made-up book. Then, I began to see something meeker. I began to see that despite the different writers and problems in the book, there is a common thread that flows through it from the Old Testament to the New Testament.

The message is simple, really, "Follow God's commandments." Once I realized that, my headache went away.

Deacon Patrick Kaprelian, *Ridgewood, New Jersey*

Living in Soul

For me, living faith is how the presence of God is working in my life. I feel that God is always present and His spirit is always moving in me, giving me insights and inspirations and ideas, but it's our choice whether we listen to them completely, partly, or not at all. The times that I've listened well, and acted accordingly, have given rise to the path I've walked that ultimately brought me to the priesthood. Everyone gets inspirations and revelations. The question is: What do you do with them when you get them?

At the age of twenty-four, I found myself living and working for a catering company in New Orleans. My job was to take food out to the men working on oil barges in the middle of the Gulf of Mexico and to bring the workers who had earned vacation time back to New Orleans. Many of these men had been on the barges for months, and the first place they wanted to go when they hit land was to the French Quarter where many lifestyles and opportunities were available.

Life was happening as it does when you are young and single. I'd go to work, come home, and go out, usually dancing with friends. In the meantime, I had visited a local Baptist church and met some of the most genuinely faithful Christian people I had ever encountered. So on one hand I was involved with a group of people of faith, and on the other hand, because of work, I was thrust into a totally opposite environment. So I was trying to figure out what was okay and what was not.

Then one evening around Easter time I was watching the movie *Jesus of Nazareth* on TV. In a sense, Jesus was right in front of me, and it suddenly struck me that if the story I was watching actually was true, then going to the French Quarter and doing drugs and drinking and sleeping with prostitutes—and all the other stuff that many of the people I knew were doing—didn't fit the plan. If the life of Jesus was true, then there is a God, and if there is a God, then I should live according to His ordinances.

Usually prayers do not get answered on the spot. God works in different ways with different people and circumstances, but on this occasion I asked God if the story of Jesus, the resurrection, the birth was true. As I prayed I got a gut feeling, an inspiration, a voice inside of me, whatever you want to term it, that said, "It's all true." From that moment on, I decided to live the straight and narrow. It wasn't too hard for me, because I wasn't a partier, in the sense of drinking and drugs anyway. Sex, we desire and do naturally, but I thought I could pretty much keep that under control, especially if I asked for God's help in tough situations. My revelation that evening did not mean the priesthood. I kept my job, but I didn't go to the French Quarter with the guys after that.

My faith started with my grandparents and parents, being taken to church, my teachers and pastors, and reading the Bible, so my faith didn't begin that day. But it was a major turning point for me. Up to then I would say that my faith was something I had been taught. From that point on, my faith was something I believed. That's when I knew God.

Embracing the resurrection was an epiphany for me… but it was only one point of the journey. Life goes on, and temptations continue to arise. The question then becomes, "Do you listen to the inspiration you had two years ago or do you go with the flow of the moment?" So, the journey continues.

Everyone comes to their faith gradually over time and in different ways. At the heart of what living faith means to me is when my heart and my mind and my soul are working as one and I can put my head on the pillow at night knowing I've been true to myself, to my faith, to my God, and that I've made decisions that reflect that knowing. At those moments I am creative and inspired and I want to go do things. I am living in the wholeness of my soul and in touch with my relationship with Jesus Christ.

†**Reverend Father Haroutiun Dagley,** *South Euclid, Ohio*

Haroutiun: The Resurrection

In the Armenian tradition, during the ordination service into the priesthood the Bishop anoints you and gives you a new first name. You don't know what your new name will be until that moment. About ten minutes before my ordination service started, the Bishop asked me if I had any requests. I told him I wanted to be ordained with the name Haroutiun. My grandfather's name was Haroutiun. My godfather's name is Haroutiun, and my father-in-law's name is Haroutiun. In Armenian Haroutiun means "resurrection."

Embracing the resurrection was the turning point in my faith, because if Jesus Christ rose from the dead then he is God and his teachings are ultimately important. If he did not, then his story is myth and Jesus was a nice moral teacher but not someone I had to pattern my life after.

I was delighted when the Bishop ordained me Haroutiun. In practical reality, inside Armenian circles the name is fine, but outside Armenian circles people have a hard time pronouncing it. Many people want to call me Father H, but how can you abbreviate the resurrection?

†**Reverend Father Haroutiun Dagley,** *South Euclid, Ohio*

Alzheimer's and the Gift of Love

Recently in my Sunday School class we were discussing the subject of love. From the Bible, we read from Corinthians 13. The passage identifies three gifts—faith, hope, and love, with love being the greatest gift of all. The children questioned the truth of that. How do we know that love is the strongest feeling, or power, or the most enduring part of a relationship? In response to their questions, I told them the story of what had happened with my mother.

About seven years ago, my mother developed Alzheimer's disease. My students knew little about the disease, so I explained that it was a progressive illness that affects the mind of the person who suffers from it. I told them that every year my mother would lose some ability to do some task she had previously taken for granted. At first, she lost the ability to write a check and balance her checkbook, then she lost the ability to cook, dress, and even feed herself. As time went on, she began to forget everybody's names as well as her own, and she could not remember who people were in relationship to her. For instance, I told them that when I visit her in the Armenian nursing home where she lives, she no longer recognizes me as her daughter or remembers my name. But, when I sit down beside her, she looks up at me, smiles, and says, "I love you."

Lynn Jamie, *Old Brookville, New York*

A Small Kindness Reaps Big Rewards

One of our parishioners, an elderly gentleman, almost never misses Sunday *Badarak*. One Sunday several weeks ago, he was absent. I asked his daughter where he was and she told me that he had had a little operation on his leg and hadn't felt well enough to attend that morning. That afternoon I picked up the phone and gave him a call. We spoke for a few minutes, during which he updated me on his health. The following Sunday he was in church as usual. When he saw me he told me how much he appreciated my call and the fact that he had been missed. Then he gave me a hug. That hug lasted me a week. A small gesture of kindness can have a big effect on someone else, and in return have a big impact back on you. If we could all do that more often it would be great.

Ara Jeknavorian, *Chelmsford, Massachusetts*

It's Never Too Late to Accept God

Although I had begun to acknowledge God as a young girl growing up in Baku, Azerbaijan, I started educating myself and growing into the faith when I came to the United States. Little by little, I began to meet and associate with people who were deeply faithful. But as I read more about God and studied the Bible with some of the people I met here, little conflicts began arising between my husband and me. At one time, I even thought of entering a nunnery. When I expressed this idea to my family, not only my husband, but also my children thought something was wrong with me, because they could not believe or accept that I could put God before them. Over time, my family began to accept the idea that God was a vital part of my life.

Then, my husband got very sick very fast. I believed in the power of prayer and in God who makes miracles and has healed many people in the past. I never stopped praying for my husband's recovery, believing that God would heal him. I prayed, but my husband died. Even though my husband was not healed physically, I believe he was healed spiritually.

When he passed away, everyone in my family, even my mother, who is a believer, said, "Where is your God now? Where was He when you needed Him?"

I had to be silent and not answer them. It seemed unbelievable to me, but God gave me the strength to face the doubts of my family. It is very hard to stand and defend yourself alone, especially among your own blood.

I am grateful because my belief in God was enough to overcome the obstacles I faced at that point in my life. I am sure that my husband is with God. We prayed together in the hospital room every day, and I hope that I helped him accept God before he passed away. We had our arguments in the past during which I told him over and over that right before death many people who had denied God all their lives come to accept Him, and that's what I believe happened. It is kind of scary.

Sometimes God takes something from us to give us something else. I would not want to say that I am grateful for my husband's death, but I have come through the situation as a stronger Christian, and for that I am grateful. Our whole life on this earth is a gift, and sometimes, as in this example, life is very short. Although my husband was taken from me, I appreciate every moment we had together, and I hope we will be together in the next life.

My main goal in life now is to be a good Christian and help bring my children and other people around me to faith by using my life and the problems that I overcame as an example.

Marietta Arzumanyan, *Belmont, Massachusetts*

Life-or-Death Decisions

In October 1994, we received the news that my husband's father had passed away in Syria. It was difficult for us to accept that we had not been able to be with him during his last days. After a month of grieving, we found out that I was pregnant. I was excited and believed that this new life was a gift to us from God in our time of sorrow.

A couple weeks into my pregnancy I learned I was carrying twins. We were delighted. My pregnancy progressed normally until early May. Coincidentally, the day of our fifth wedding anniversary, I felt odd. The next morning my water broke and I went into labor. That evening I delivered twins, a boy and a girl. Both babies were premature and underdeveloped. The doctors wanted to put them on ventilators and other life-support machines.

The doctors were not sure they could save the twins, but they were sure that even if they did, the babies would never live normal lives. It was a hard decision to make. My husband and I chose to let them breathe on their own for as long as they could and to accept that if their lives were to end, they would end.

That was one of the hardest days of my life.

I witnessed my tiny twins' labored breathing as they lay in their cribs next to my bed in the hospital room. I held them and went through the early mothering tasks with each of them. Our priest came and we named and christened them. They each lived about six hours. I was by their side when they took their last breaths.

Watching them die was hard, but arranging cemetery plots and burying them was even harder. My father-in-law had died, and now the twins were dead, too. I knew that God had done this for a reason, but I did not know what the reason was.

A year later, I discovered I was pregnant again. I was excited, but this time I was also afraid. Then, the doctor heard three heartbeats. An ultrasound showed three sacks. I was pregnant with natural triplets. My fear tripled with the news. All I could think about was what I had gone through with the twins.

A week later, at my next appointment, the doctor told my husband and me that based on my history of premature labor, chances were high that I would deliver prematurely again. He strongly recommended that I abort two of the three babies with the hope that the remaining baby would survive.

We were stunned. I have always been against abortion.

Now, a doctor I trusted was telling me that if I wanted a healthy, normal child, aborting two of the three fetuses would be the best thing to do.

We sat and listened as best we could as the doctor explained the procedure. At the end of that meeting he asked us to sign consent forms he had prepared to go ahead with the procedure. I told him that we needed some time to think about it and that we would call him in a week. In the car on the ride home we asked ourselves, How could we take the lives of two babies? Which two would be taken? What if we aborted two and the remaining one died? What if we left all three and lost all three?

What-if scenarios played over and over in my mind. The possibility of losing five babies was horrifying. I needed an answer. Had the doctor given me an absolute it might have made things easier, but he had only strongly recommended the abortions. I prayed to God for an answer and the openness to stay aware of His guidance.

I discussed the situation with my parents and Der Hayr and Yeretzgin Paulette. Paulette helped me walk through my fears one night at their home, because my mind was racing from one catastrophic outcome to another. I feared that the triplets would be born prematurely and they would live but be handicapped with crippling birth defects. I was afraid that I would go into premature labor and lose all three. I began to lean towards following the advice of the doctor.

I wanted someone to tell me what to do. But no one could do that. I had to make the final decision myself, and the time to decide ticked nearer.

I drove home praying for a sign from God to help me with the decision. I cried and cried all night. Finally I slept a little. The next morning I woke knowing what I had to do. I knew in my heart and gut that there was a reason God gave me three, and if anything were going to happen I would rather it happen on its own than by my hand.

I decided to see the pregnancy through to its natural conclusion—whatever that might be.

That afternoon when the doctor called I told him that I had decided not to go through with the procedure. "What do you mean you are not going to go through with it?" he said. I told him I believed that God gave me three babies for a reason and if I took the lives of two of these babies and saved one, I would always live with the pain of that decision. I told him I felt strongly that these three were meant to be together and I believed this pregnancy would be okay.

Two days later the doctor called me back. He told me he was glad I had made that decision. He said he respected me as a person of faith and he would support me in what I was doing. Hearing that from the doctor gave me courage. I really felt then that I had made the right decision.

It was a very tough pregnancy, beginning with doctor visits every week. At four months I was one centimeter dilated and started to get contractions. At twenty-two weeks I was hospitalized for 24/7 bed rest. Those days in the hospital were the slowest days of my life, but I didn't have any fear. I felt that things would be fine. I would wake up, mark another day off the calendar, lie in bed, and pray. I prayed for the health of my babies and for me to go as long as I could. Nine weeks later I gave birth to triplets—two boys and a girl. They weighed 2.5, 2.75, and 3 pounds. They were all healthy. They did not need oxygen, ventilators, or machines. They did need to gain weight and learn how to suck the bottle on their own.

Nazaret Setrak, Hrant Hagop, and Melanie Alice will be four years old soon. I know God gave me these three beautiful, healthy children for a reason. I dare not speculate why. Three at once is a lot of work. But I'm grateful. They are a miracle.

Talin Nalbandian, *Troy, New York*

Snow Is My Sign from God

Der Hayr and I had been married for about six months when the Bishop asked him to continue his studies at the Seminary in Jerusalem. At the time we were living in New York City. I had started my own successful business, and I was commuting to Massachusetts on the weekends because my mother was sick. All things considered, I really didn't want to go to Jerusalem. I didn't think it was the right thing for me to do personally, but I felt I had to go. Der Hayr was my husband. I agreed with his ministry, and I wanted to be as supportive as I could be, so we went to Jerusalem.

But in Jerusalem, even after I had unpacked and was trying to settle in, in my mind I was still saying, "I don't want to be here. I could have continued my business. My mother is sick. She needs me closer." I honestly didn't think I could stay. I prayed and prayed to God asking him to show me a sign that I should be in Jerusalem.

One day, while Der Hayr and I were exploring the city on foot, we noticed the clouds darkening and the day growing colder. Then, it started to snow. The people of Jerusalem were amazed. Jerusalem enjoys a very warm climate, so many of them did not know what snow was. It had not snowed there in more than fifty years.

I grew up in Massachusetts and I had always loved the snow. As those big white flakes fell from the Jerusalem sky, I knew that this was my sign from God. The snowflakes were telling me that I was in the right place for me as a person and for us as a newly wedded couple. We stayed in Jerusalem for eight months, studying at the Seminary. After that snowfall, my heart and mind were at peace and it was a wonderful experience.

We returned to the United States, and our son was born in Milwaukee, Wisconsin. St. Gregory the Illuminator Armenian Church in Haverhill, Massachusetts, was our first parish. We were close to family and friends, and things were good. It snowed there and we were very happy. Then my husband decided it was time to move on with his ministry. He spoke to the Bishop, and the possibility of serving a parish in California was discussed. I definitely did not want to move to California. By this time, my mother was very ill. We had two sons, and I did not want to take them away from the family they knew.

But Der Hayr was given a parish in California. Again, I wanted to support my husband's ministry, so we moved. While unpacking in California, I felt very much as I had when unpacking in Jerusalem. This time I felt more strongly that we had made the right decision to come, but in the back of my mind I was saying, "This is California—3000 miles away from my family." Again, I prayed for a sign from God that this was where we should be at this point in our lives.

One morning, not long after we had arrived, the phone rang. It was very early, about 5:30 in the morning. "Look out the window," the caller said. "It's snowing." It had not snowed in the valley for forty years. When I saw those snowflakes I knew that they were my sign. From that moment on, I knew we would be comfortable in California and that California was to be our home, at least for now.

Yeretzgin Lana Kaishian, Yettem, California

Snowflakes

As a priest, as a husband, as a father, I know how hard it is to work daily devotional prayer into your schedule. I can't say I do it every day, but I do know the value of it.

One way I pray is by taking a walk. I find that walking clears or shifts my attention from what I have to do at the parish council meeting, or what I plan to do with the toddler group this week, or where I'm going to put the lantern for the Receiving the Light service. I especially enjoy walking in the snow when it's snowing. I start out thinking about the things I have to do, and, inevitably, the snow coming down catches my eye and, instead of thinking about those things, I start watching the falling snowflakes. I may notice that the snowflakes are white, and that makes me think about God's holiness, or, because I can't see where they are coming from, it makes me consider God's vastness, or I remember from science class that every snowflake has a different shape, and, in remembering that fact, I think about how God touches everything in different ways yet works in harmony with everything. From there I begin to let go of all those tasks I was thinking about, and I begin opening up to His presence.

†Reverend Father Haroutiun Dagley, *South Euclid, Ohio*

Holding the Little Cross

I attended a spiritual retreat Father Yeprem held at a retreat center one weekend. At the end of the retreat, Father Yeprem brought out the special cloth and little cross inlaid with stones that he carries with him as he walks past the congregation at the beginning of the *Badarak* service and announced that he was going to pass it around to every person at the retreat. My heart skipped a beat, because I had always thought that one day I would like to just touch that little cross with my hands. When it came to my turn, I held it, and I cried. I had never felt that I would be worthy enough to hold that cross. But I was.

Pat Paragamian, *Racine, Wisconsin*

Prodigal Son

I have three children. After twenty-six years of marriage, my husband left the family. My oldest son was especially troubled and angry about his father's leaving, and, soon after, he too walked away from the family. My son was not on drugs or alcohol; he was just trying to work his way through some family issues. To do that, he needed to separate himself completely from his brother, his sister, and me.

I did an awful lot of crying and grieving during those years he was gone. My feelings of loss and hopelessness were especially intense on his birthdays. On one birthday, not long after he left, I started to write. It helped to explore on paper some of the really hard-to-deal-with feelings I was having. Through my writing, and after many hours of counseling, I learned to live with the situation by turning it over to God. "Let go and let God" became my motto. Then, during a counseling session just before the New Year eleven years after my son had left, it suddenly hit me: I didn't know how and I didn't know when, but I knew my son was coming home.

One Sunday morning three months later, I stumbled down a couple of steps and twisted my ankle. The injury was bad enough that I decided not go to church that morning. While I was puttering around the kitchen, the doorbell rang. I opened the door and saw my long-lost son standing there. At first I couldn't quite grasp that it was him. The painful years melted away as we hugged and cried and uttered mutual regrets and apologies. He asked for my forgiveness. I said, "You don't have to ask for forgiveness. I love you." He said, "Yes, I do. I have to know that you know that I am sorry." Our reunion was the most enchanting, delightful experience of my life. I shall never forget it.

It is many years later now. I'm sorry we lost so much precious time to be together, but I've learned to begin again, from that day, and to leave the past behind me. I have since received many wonderful notes and cards from my son, thanking me for allowing him the space to grow and find himself. It makes me feel that the pain we endured was somehow worthwhile. And, a positive came out of the estrangement. Initially I began writing as a way to console myself, but I continue to write today and have discovered that writing is my passion.

Gloria Semonian, *Royal Oak, Michigan*

Paul's Back

I grew up in Watertown, Massachusetts, when Watertown was very Armenian. Without question, the church and my faith were an important and dear part of my life. Like my friends, I attended Armenian School, Sunday School, and Armenian Church Youth Organization at St. James Armenian Church. St. James was "where the action was" in town. Even my Irish buddies came. To this day we laugh when they use Armenian words. The Armenian community in Watertown was vibrant and influential. We assimilated our non-Armenian neighbors.

When I graduated from Watertown High School I stayed local. Keeping my ties with family and friends was more important than following a curriculum that required attending a school someplace other than the immediate area. I went to Bentley College, earned a business degree, and stayed in touch with the people I had developed relationships with while growing up in Watertown.

After college, I married my college-era sweetheart. She was Armenian, too. Her family was local and religious. Our marriage lasted four years. My divorce is where my life and my story begin, because at that time I felt that my faith had let me down.

On one level I could see the reasons that led to our separation, but all the time our marriage was breaking up I was hoping that the bonds of our common faith and heritage would prevail and we would figure out a way to have a traditional Armenian marriage. Like my parents did. Like her parents did. Those were my role models.

To this day I'll never forget my thought as I walked out of that divorce court: I did everything correctly and it didn't work out.

I was angry and unhappy. I felt that God had let me down. In that frame of mind, I went about my business and started dating again. At the age of thirty, I met the woman who would become my second wife. She was not religious, nor was her family very religious. She was a person who was challenging life and tradition. When I got involved with her I also got involved with a group of people who were not only questioning whether or not there is a God, but questioning whether or not family was where you got your best love.

This new group fed right into my state of mind at the time. I felt I had to challenge the faith and values of my upbringing. I wanted to address those essential questions and to decide what I believed for myself. I had seen the hypocrisies of the church firsthand. I'd seen how many of the priests and those involved with the administration of the church were out for themselves and not for the community. People talk about God, people worship God, people praise God, but there are all kinds of hypocrisy. I had seen the dark side of the faith and, on top of everything else, I had a failed Armenian marriage.

I married my second wife, and, throughout my thirties, I challenged my faith. I lived a life completely outside of the Armenian-Watertown world. I disassociated myself from the church. I disassociated myself from the majority of my friends. I even decided not to see my family as often. I let the pendulum swing to the opposite extreme.

I was supposed to be happy, but I wasn't. Things were missing. I could not bring myself to believe that there wasn't a God. Somewhere, down deep, I felt that there was. It took me several years to realize that I didn't want to lose the faith, my family, and the community of people I had left behind.

I'll be honest. I have not come full-circle. Part of me still believes there is no God, but I've also realized that it isn't important. What is important is the sense of what is being communicated. What's important are the teachings of Jesus Christ. Even while I was actively questioning the existence of Jesus or of God, I never left behind the teachings of my faith. It took me years, but I finally realized that the group of people I was associated with were angry, too. My second marriage didn't last much longer.

By then I was into my forties. Luckily, I met a wonderful woman. She is not Armenian, but she was married to an Armenian before me. She wanted to put her stakes down and build a home and that's what I wanted right from the start. We now have a beautiful daughter, and everything feels right.

When Father Dajad married me—the third time—he kept saying over and over again, "Paul's back. He's back." It's good to be back.

Paul Pogharian, *Watertown, Massachusetts*

The Devil in One Ear and the Angel in the Other

I'm a married priest. Every day it seems I'm reminded of the Mills Brothers' song that says, "You always hurt the one you love most of all." It's the little things like when you are having a conversation with your wife and you know you should say one thing but you don't. Instead of being loving you throw in a dig and immediately you're sorry you said it.

The opportunity to listen and know God's will for us is always present. The spirit is willing but the flesh is weak. We all do and say things that we know are wrong, but we do them anyway. The key is to try to listen and walk in harmony with God. That's what I think of when I think of the living faith. It's not easy for any of us, including priests.

†Reverend Father Haroutiun Dagley, *South Euclid, Ohio*

Getting Out of the Way

What keeps my faith alive is often just getting myself out of my own way. I think we block our own light. Our fears, our distrust, and our need for control—these are the things that close in and suffocate God's voice within us.

Sometimes it takes me until the flame almost flickers out before I remember to open up and let God and others back in. I do this through prayer and meditation. I wouldn't call it a process; I call it a relationship and opening myself up to that relationship. Part of it is letting go of whatever I thought or think is so important, because relative to that relationship it never is.

We often hear how at any given moment we use only a small percentage of our brains. I am convinced we use even less of our souls. Getting out of my own way is a matter of mindfulness.

Jason Demerjian, *Waltham, Massachusetts*

Don't Cry, Son

I was a schoolboy when my father was dying. I knew he was very ill. I prayed that he would recover, but it didn't help.

One day while I was with him in his room I started to cry. He said, "Don't cry, son. God's been good to me. I went through the Genocide. I never expected to have a family, and I never thought that I would see a life like I have seen here in America. I've lived thirty-five years and every one of those years has been a bonus, because I should have been dead."

Richard Hagopian, Visalia, California

Fear of Death

Growing up I suffered from a fear of death. In particular, I was afraid of flying in airplanes, because I felt I was going to die in a plane crash. I forced myself to take plane trips, but I was paranoid about them. Then when I got married, my fear of death became even stronger.

Soon after we were married my husband was scheduled to go on a business trip by plane. "What if something happens to you?" I asked him.

My husband looked at me. "Isn't it enough that you and I have known each other?"

I looked back at him dumbfounded. It took a long while for the meaning of what he said to sink in.

I got on an airplane with my husband and our young son for the first time recently. As we boarded, I felt nervous and scared. But once we were seated, I looked at the two of them and realized that I had nothing to be afraid of because what my husband had said was true. I had married a man I consider my soulmate. We live a wonderful, happy life together. I have a beautiful, healthy family, and the friends I have I love very much. So if anything were to happen right now, I would leave this world content. There was no reason to fear what would happen next because everything that I needed to happen had already happened.

Amazingly, I don't fear flying anymore. And I certainly don't have the fear of death I had before.

Rachel Onanian Nadjarian, Ann Arbor, Michigan

I Want to Go Now, Mary

I had two wonderful sisters. Both died of breast cancer. I have breast cancer also, but I am a survivor. That makes three of us with the same disease. My sister, Marge, died at the age of thirty-nine. My other sister, Sue, passed away a few years ago. Her passing was very difficult for me. She was my best friend.

During her final days, Sue was very ill. Fortunately, we were able to keep her home with her family. She was not on any medication. She was not delirious. She was not in pain.

On her final afternoon, Sue called me over to her side. "Why am I not dying? I want to go now," she whispered. I wasn't sure she knew what she was saying, so I asked her who I was. "You're my sister, Mary," she replied.

"Do you know that your children are all here, around you?"

"Yes. I do," she said. "But, they want me to come now and I want to go. What is taking so long? What's holding me up?"

"Sue, who do you see?" I asked.

"Mom is there. I see Dad. Someone else is calling me, too. I want to go. What is taking so long, Mary?"

How can we not believe in a power greater than ourselves? Family was very important to my sister, but even with her children around her, she did not care. She wanted to go. I believe that my sister witnessed something greater than herself. That evening she passed away with the nicest smile on her face.

Mary Stevoff, *Chicago, Illinois*

Cancer: A Story from Four Perspectives

A Mother's Perspective

Today is my daughter's birthday. I lost her to ovarian cancer ten years ago July. She would have been forty today.

The year after she was diagnosed with ovarian cancer, I was diagnosed with ovarian cancer. My cancer has responded to treatment, but my daughter suffered for two years. She lost her kidneys, and finally she passed away.

It is very difficult to believe in God when you live through tragedies like this. I questioned my faith because I felt that we were good people. We always worked for the church. We did the right things. We were honest with everyone. My husband and I both had a very difficult time coping. "Why did this happen to us?" we asked.

It took time, but finally we came to realize that this happens to other people too. They say that when God goes to the rose garden he always takes the prettiest roses. That was true when He picked my daughter. It was very difficult to go back to church, but, with the help of Father Kevork, slowly we returned and redeemed our faith.

Marge Esraelian, *Selma, California*

* * *

An Aunt's Perspective

I have had two nieces die of cancer. It is very painful to witness young women you love and have known lose their lives to such a debilitating illness. Then I got cancer. When I was diagnosed with the disease, my nieces became my anchors. I realized that if they could be called from this earth, why would I be any different? The courage they had showed during their battle with the disease gave me the strength to go through my illness. They were both very brave. Why should I not be? Their bravery made me a lot braver in facing my own cancer than I could ever have been without their examples.

We are all going to go—one way or another. Instead of feeling bitter that I lost my nieces too early in life, I am thankful that I got to know them. I learned a lot from them when they were alive, and they became my role models when I faced my own mortality. Today, I am a cancer survivor. Every day I thank God for what I have and for the time I had with both of those fine young women.

Lorraine Esraelian, *Fowler, California*

* * *

A Cousin's Perspective

Shortly before Gail died, her sister Pam gave birth to twins. Everyone knew Pam was pregnant. She had gone to the doctor for regular checkups. The doctor had said that the child had a strong heartbeat, and everyone expected a single child.

In the delivery room, Pam gave birth to a baby boy they named Bret. The doctor was cleaning up and had left the room when Pam asked the nurse to get him back, because something was not right. The doctor came back in, and, sure enough, a second child was born. This surprise baby was a girl they christened Heather.

Gail and Heather were very close in the brief time that they had together. Gail often spoke of the little girl's orneriness. To this day, my uncle often calls Heather "Gail." I think that when he looks at his granddaughter, he sees his daughter, Gail.

I just made a connection. It just occurred to me that God might have given this second child, whom no one contemplated at the time, to the family as a gift, knowing that we would soon lose Gail.

Tom Miles, *Fresno, California*

* * *

A Visitor's Perspective

It was January shortly after Armenian Christmas. I was a seminarian at the time, and I was visiting a parish in California where my wife's family lived. A family in the parish had not celebrated American Christmas or Armenian Christmas. The daughter had cancer, and, at the same time, she was battling this illness, her mother was diagnosed with the same type of cancer. The family was struggling with the illnesses, the chemotherapy, and the radiation treatments. However, they felt they had to celebrate Christmas because there were small children in the family, but none of them had the desire to celebrate. Honestly, who would?

Their priest, Father Kevork Arakelian, found out that the family had decided to get together to exchange a few gifts and share a meal that Saturday, January 12. He wanted to do something special for the family, but he wasn't sure what to do. Then an idea came to him. Father Kevork called his parishioners and asked them to gather that afternoon a few blocks from where the family lived. We met about twenty other members of the parish on the street corner that afternoon. Father Kevork handed out Christmas carol books and we decided what songs we wanted to sing. Then we walked to the family's home singing carols. We sang "O Come All Ye Faithful" as the family opened the door.

Everyone began to cry…the family and all of us. They invited us in, and Father Kevork performed a home blessing. We brought Christmas to their household on that otherwise very ordinary day, and the family said that it was the best Christmas anyone could ask for.

Reverend Father Stepanos Doudoukjian, *Latham, New York*

A Road Less Traveled

I didn't want to just frequent the church. I wanted to make it an everyday experience.

Back in the early 1980s, I approached the Primate about entering the Armenian priesthood. St. Nersess Seminary had not opened yet, so I attended a Greek Orthodox seminary. After a couple of years, St. Nersess opened, and I spent the next two years studying there. It was a difficult period. The school was newly formed and in transition. I was somebody who lacked discipline and formation in my life. The combination made it so things just didn't work out as I had hoped. With the seminary's consent, I returned home to Worcester, Massachusetts, with the idea that I would finish my undergraduate studies and possibly return to the seminary.

But my life took a different twist. Back in my hometown, I met up with some friends who invited me to join a rock-and-roll band they were putting together. In no time at all, I was singing in a heavy-metal band. Little by little my hair grew longer, and my physical appearance changed.

For the next five years I sang in the band, and it became a successful venture. Most of that time I was physically removed from the church and associated with people who were not the most God-fearing people. Many professed atheism. A few even claimed that they were warlocks and looking into magic. It was a challenge for me to keep my faith.

Often while singing on stage, as the words of a song were coming out of my mouth, I was thinking, what am I doing here? This is not me. Yet, there was an attraction to it. Every day I prayed that God would keep his eye on me and keep me from going too far over the edge with the whole lifestyle.

Things went well, maybe too well. I began to feel that if I continued to stay with the band its success might lock me onto that path. I was at a crossroads.

Years before, after I had left the seminary and before I joined the band, I had met two nuns who belonged to a Catholic monastic community in southern Canada. They had given me some literature about the monastery, which I had stuffed in a drawer. Five years later, I opened that drawer and read the literature again.

Monasticism appealed to me. The idea behind monasticism is to totally separate from the world and to consecrate yourself to God by uniting yourself to Him. Some people argue that monasticism conflicts with being a Christian because they think Christianity is best lived within the framework of society. But, for others, moving away from a worldly life with all its distractions moves them closer to God. I knew also that monasticism was an accepted tradition in the Armenian Church. I called a friend who I thought might be interested in learning more about the monastery, and together we drove to Canada to check it out.

It did not take me long to learn that I needed and wanted to be there. I returned home and told my parents that I had decided to join the monastery. I quit the band, gave away all of my personal possessions, cut my hair, and returned to the Catholic monastic community in Canada.

I stayed for almost twelve years. When I was in the band, I went to bed around 4:00 a.m. At the monastery, that's when I had to get up. My whole life went into reverse mode. Initially it was difficult to adapt to those changes, both physically and emotionally.

Another aspect of monastic life that took some getting used to was doing everything in community. We participated in prayer and ate all our meals together. We worked during the day. The monastery was self-contained. We had our own gardens and farmed, we made our own clothes, and we logged our own wood and ran a sawmill. We did our own construction, including the electricity and plumbing. We operated our own print shop. There was a lot to do, and our days were very busy.

And there was no leaving the monastery except on rare occasions when you went out on monastery business. For twelve years I could not go home for any reason. I missed many important family events, like weddings and funerals, which was difficult. My parents were allowed to visit once a month, but the monastery was a nine hour drive from Worcester. Heroically, they visited me four or five times a year.

In the monastery, I began to appreciate and understand the Gospel in a way I never had before. Everything I learned was in line with the traditional teaching of the Armenian Church. This was important for me, because I would not participate in any group that was questionable with regard to how they taught and practiced the faith. Nothing at the monastery opposed anything I had been brought up to believe. My whole way of looking at things through the Gospel and through living a monastic life transformed how I felt about my faith, especially as an Armenian Christian.

Although I was physically distant from the Armenian Church, I found myself increasingly drawn to it and the practices of my origin. Not a moment seemed to go by when I wasn't praying for the Armenian Church. Daily I prayed that God would someday, somehow, bring me back to it better prepared to serve. I became starved for things Armenian. I begged people to send me the *Reporter*, the *Mirror-Spectator*, *AIM Magazine*, and anything else with Armenian news. They did, and I spent much of my spare time cutting and pasting together scrapbooks covering every aspect of the life of the Armenian Church from the beginning to the present. As my scrapbooks grew in number and volume, so grew my love and yearning for the church of my childhood.

Then I received an invitation to my brother's wedding. Enclosed with the invitation was a note asking that I be allowed to attend the wedding and serve as a deacon. Although the request was contrary to the tradition of the monastery, the Superior of the Monastery came to the retreat house where I was working. He showed me the letter, and asked me if I wanted to go. I knew from past experience that it was best not to seem too gung-ho. The Superior left saying that he would think about the request and get back to me in a couple of weeks. Nothing moves quickly in a monastery. A couple of weeks later he came by and told me that they had decided to send me to my brother's wedding. To my delight, it turned out that my first visit home after more than a decade would last three weeks.

Before the wedding, and almost two decades after I had expressed my initial desire to enter the Armenian priesthood, I was invited by the Primate to visit the Diocese in New York to discuss the possibility of ordination. The Primate and I came to an agreement, and I returned to the monastery to discuss the offer with them. The Superior gave me his blessing, and I left the monastery amicably with the doors open to me if I ever wanted to return.

I walked out of the monastery grateful for the invaluable gift they had given me that I might not have received anywhere else.

Deacon Francis K. Merzigian, *New York, New York*

Smile That Smile

One Sunday I was visiting the Armenian protestant church in Belmont, Massachusetts. The guest speaker that morning was an ex-convict named Jesse. He was encouraging people to visit the prisons and to attend services with the inmates at the prison chapel. He seemed to speak from the heart, and he inspired me. I went up to meet him afterwards and told him that I would like to go with him to the prison chapel. After that I began to worship there quite often.

During one visit to the prison chapel, I met a man who went by the name of Doctor Love. He played the piano. When he played and sang, it was as if God were singing through him. At one point, he asked us to sing along with him. We joined in. A bar or two later, he stopped playing. "No," he shouted. "That ain't right before God," I guess we sounded a little off key. God's joy was present in Doctor Love's music. I can't play and sing like that, so his way of expressing God's joy was something I could appreciate, but not something I could emulate.

Another time Jesse was offering the message. He got up and began to talk about Job. Jesse brought the story of Job's sacrifice alive in a way that I have never forgotten. I felt Job's pain. I felt his questioning God—Why? Why? Why? Best of all, as Jesse told the story, he smiled this incredible smile. When I saw that smile on his face I said to myself, I want to smile that smile because God smiled through his smile. Over the years a few people have told me that they've been touched by something I've done. My smile is different than Jesse's smile, but it feels good to know that in some way I've smiled that smile for others to see.

†Reverend Father Haroutiun Dagley, *South Euclid, Ohio*

An Old Georgian Woman

I work as an associate producer in New York City. Last January, while working on the production of the documentary, "The Armenians: A Story of Survival" for Public Television, I was in Tbilisi, Georgia. The once prosperous and vibrant Armenian community in Tbilisi is suffering badly. Their money has run out, and there are no jobs. It's very sad.

One day, we visited St. Kevork, the main Armenian monastery in the city, to shoot some footage. It was late in the afternoon when we arrived. Outside, it was freezing cold. Inside the church, it wasn't much warmer. We were filming as the lady who cleaned the floors and the lady who sold the candles were preparing to close the church for the night. Then an old woman who looked like someone we would call a bag lady walked in. She looked like a typical Armenian grandmother, except that her face was black and blue. She wore a jacket tied closed with a piece of rope.

Our churches in that part of the world don't generally have pews. This church had two. She headed straight for the closest pew, saying, "This is where I'm going to sleep tonight." I watched as the two ladies who worked in the church exchanged glances. It was obvious that they knew this woman as someone who came in once in a while. "You can't stay here," they told her. "You'll freeze. Besides we are closing up. Don't you have somewhere to go?"

"No. No. I'm going to sleep here tonight. No worries. No worries." The old woman waved them away as she sat down on the pew. Then she pulled a frozen soggy piece of bread out of a plastic bag she had hidden under her coat. She looked up at me, held out the bread, and said in perfect Armenian, "There is a little heater over there. Put this on the heater. We will eat some bread." As she held the bread towards me, I noticed her hands were frozen in a crumbled, wrinkled way.

I was speechless. Here was this old woman, on the verge of starving, who was inviting me to share her bread. The ladies quickly filled the silence by telling me that she had no home or family as far as they knew and that her mind was not completely there.

"Grandma," I said finally. "What happened to you? Your face is covered with bruises."

"Oh, I get dizzy. I fall on my face. It happens often," she said in a light-hearted way, as if it was no big deal. I was so blown away that I turned to the church ladies and told them I wanted to give her some money. They said that she did not understand the concept of a $20 bill and would lose it or someone on the street would say it's worth a bottle of water. They would sell her the water and take the money. That's what she would get out of a gift of money.

I knew they were right, but I desperately wanted to do something for this Georgian-born and -raised Armenian grandmother who spoke beautiful Armenian. My heart was breaking. Finally it occurred to me that since we were in church we could light a candle together. She agreed and got up from the bench. Taking little inch steps, we made it to the candle stand and together we lit a candle. Then she pushed me out of her way. Honestly, I was a bit offended. I thought, What is she doing now? I was practically in tears I was so emotional.

I stood back and watched her shuffle towards the altar. She went around the little wood railing that separated the rest of the church from the altar. Underneath the altar in traditional Armenian churches is a *khatchkar*, a cross, which faces the church. I watched as this old woman who routinely passed out, falling flat on her face, got down on her knees, made the sign of the cross, said a prayer, and kissed the cross under the altar. She had so much trouble standing back up I had to help her to her feet. "Okay," she said. "Now I need somewhere to sleep."

I was amazed. I couldn't understand why it had been so important to her to live out every single aspect of what she felt she was expected to do when she lit a candle. Not just light a candle and say a prayer, but go to the altar, get on her knees, and kiss the cross.

My boss, who was not Armenian, was standing in the background, saying, "Oh, this is incredible footage." But then he heard me crying. For the first time during the trip I broke down completely. I didn't know what to do. I wanted to hold her. I wanted to take her home with me. How could any human being suffer as much as this grandma was suffering? And yet, what had she done? She had gotten on her knees and thanked God for her life. I pulled my gloves and scarf out my backpack and gave them to her. She thanked me and blessed me as if I were a blood relative.

That Georgian-Armenian grandma amazed me with her faith and with her ability to survive. Her religion, her culture, and her language had survived through the years both good and bad.

Shant Petrossian, *New York, New York*

Pass It Forward

One of my favorite prayers is the part of the Liturgy when we pray that we will be given the time to do good. Living in Armenia, the opportunity to help people happens often.

It's the day that you see a bunch of kids playing and they want to fix up their playground area so you get a few of your friends together and you help them to fix it up. Then two weeks later you pass by and find that they are taking care of it themselves without any assistance at all.

Or, it's the day that a neighbor who has a sick child comes to you and says, "We're in a terrible situation. We don't know what we are going to do for this kid." And you help out in a very minimal way, really. Then for weeks afterwards the family seems restored. They behave differently. They are more friendly and you notice them taking time out to help other people.

When you do good for someone, they do good for someone else. It becomes a chain.

Tom Samuelian, *Yerevan, Armenia*

The Almond Seed

Early in my ministry, I used to visit an old woman living in a nursing home in the Boston area. She was born in Harpout and had gone through the massacres. Toward the end of her life, when I walked into her room, her mind transported her back to the old country and she thought I was her priest in Harpout. "Der Hayr," she said on one visit, "Yesterday my father and I planted an almond seed in the backyard. Can we walk outside now to see if it has grown?"

Getting this woman outside posed a difficult task. She could barely walk. Her room was on the second floor, and, even if I could get her outside, the nursing home was located on a highway with cars flying by. What little yard there was, was gravel. At the time it seemed to me that our chance of ending up as road kill was higher than the chance of her seeing an almond tree sprouting out of stones.

But you know what? I wish I had taken her outside that day. Today I know in my heart that that dear lady would have seen a spouting tree, because she still had hope. She still had faith that if she planted an almond seed in the earth, God would show her a miraculous sign.

Reverend Father Yeprem Kelegian, *Racine, Wisconsin*

Tiny Increments of Hope and Progress

My faith was tested when I became ill. I have a recurring disease for which there is no cure. One morning I woke up and couldn't raise my head off the pillow. It was scary. Once I got over the initial shock of my diagnosis, I had to learn how to live with it.

I learned to break down previously simple tasks into doable increments. If I couldn't get out of bed that morning, then my task for that day was to try to get out of bed. If I couldn't make dinner that night, then my task was to try to put together a meal for the family that evening. Teaching myself to work in tiny increments was very difficult and challenging at first. I really had to push myself. It wasn't easy, but I did it.

I also learned that if I was going to get through this, I had to go to my Bible every day and ground myself in my faith. I learned too that one of the best ways to get better is to help other people affected by the same disease. People call me on the phone and I try to help them work through their problems. I try to give them hope. I tell them that I am better. Not that I am well, but that I am better. I work with them so that they begin to think positively, learn to break their daily tasks into tiny increments like I did, and realize that there is strength to be found in the Bible. Mostly, I find that people just want to talk. I listen. I am a good listener.

I expect to be sick again, so my faith will be tested again. When that day comes, when that morning arrives when I cannot get my head off the pillow, will I say, "I can't do this"? Or will I go to my Bible and reestablish myself in my faith?

†**Carla Donobedian,** *Fresno, California*

You Go On

My faith was tested many years ago when our five-year-old son was diagnosed with leukemia. I was so grateful that I was brought up in a home where religion was preached and lived. My faith in Jesus Christ kept me strong through the yearlong illness and the death of our little boy. He was an angel, and I believe we will meet again some day. I was able to thank God for his life, short as it was, and because of my faith I didn't have bitter feelings that other people's children were not taken. Years later, our daughters married and we have three grandsons. So things work out. You go on.

Vi Selvian, *Fresno, California*

Turn to God with Hope

There have been some very bad times in my life. I remember one time, back in 1975, when I had just learned from the doctor that my wife had only two months to live. I was badly shaken. She was in the hospital and was not responding to the medication. Our children were young.

I went to St. John the Divine in Manhattan. Suddenly, while walking from one chapel to the other, I was consoled by a phrase that had suddenly come into my mind. In Armenian it is a verse from a psalm, *Housa ar Asdvadz*: Turn to God with hope. I repeated it over and over again to myself.

As I left the cathedral I realized that I was totally relieved from the pressures that had brought me there. When I arrived home, the doctor called with the wonderful news that my wife had begun to respond to the medication. She pulled through. We enjoyed each other's companionship for another fourteen years, and she was able to take care of the children until they were old enough to understand and cope with her passing.

Very Reverend Father Krikor Maksoudian, *Arlington, Massachusetts*

Balaam's* Donkey

My mother went through the massacre. She lost her husband, her home, and most of her family. Throughout her life, my mother held the donkey in very high regard. I thought her reverence for donkeys was strange until one day she told me this story.

The old country where she was from was very mountainous. During the deportation, my mother, her mother, and her sister were traveling at the head of the caravans of Armenians being driven into the desert by the Turks. The few possessions they had were loaded on the back of the family donkey. One day, the caravans were traveling across a steep mountainous area on a road that was so narrow only one-way traffic could pass when a Turkish military caravan traveling in the opposite direction met them head on. The Turks tried to push the Armenian caravan off the mountain so that they could pass, but our family donkey was in the lead. When the Turks tried to push the donkey off the ledge, the donkey planted its four feet on the ground, stood solid as a rock, and refused to budge. The Turks jabbed and jabbed him with their swords, but the donkey held firm. The Turks cursed the donkey and the caravans of Armenians behind it, but in the end they were forced to go back the way they came. Because of that donkey, every Armenian in the caravans was saved. To this day, whenever I see a donkey I think of my mother in a very loving way.

Gloria Semonian, *Royal Oak, Michigan*

---

* Numbers 22

A Lesson in Patience

I have never lost my faith, but at times I've forgotten what pocket it was in. I worked in mortgage banking for fifteen years before entering the seminary. Mortgage banking is a competitive business packed with pressure. It was fun, but there was plenty of opportunity for emotions to get out of control.

My partner and I were working hard to finance a large loan for a broker on Long Island. We had gotten some business from this broker before and wanted more from him in the future, so we tried to be as competitive as possible. At the eleventh hour, the broker's customer announced that he had gotten a better deal somewhere else and the loan fell through.

I was upset. My income was based on commissions I earned from closed loans only. I had lost a lot of money on this loan and over a month's worth of work. I remember throwing the folder against my office wall and shouting, "God, what did you do this for? I worked really hard on this loan."

Hearing myself made me stop. I knew better. I got mad at God and I got mad at the person I thought did me wrong rather than praying for that person. I forced myself back to work, but at lunch I sat in my car with my eyes closed still thinking about what had happened.

A week later the broker on Long Island called to offer me two much easier loans to finance. Then he said, "Don't feel bad. The loan we lost fell though with the other broker, too." Come to find out, the customer had falsified documents. It made me realize that I'm not smarter than God. I don't have all the facts. Since then I've had much more patience with everything. Losing that loan taught me that I am really here just for the ride and that I'm going to learn from God.

Deacon Mitchell Mouradjian, *New Rochelle, New York*

Keeping Honest

I travel a lot both in the car and on airplanes. As a result I have a lot of time for reading and thinking. I sometimes feel that this is the time I am the most alone, but it is also the time when I feel most comfortable. It's the time I have to reflect on not just what has to be done, but on who I am and how I've worked through the challenges of situations.

A few years ago, the company I founded went public. The previous challenges and obligations of running a successful company escalated into helping to run a company successfully in the eyes of shareholders. Since then I find myself not just asking who I am as a leader of a publicly traded company, but who I am as a person and what I am contributing to the greater good. I try to keep honest with the latter and not just the former. It can very easily get away from you if you don't stop and ask yourself those types of questions.

James Kalustian, *Arlington, Massachusetts*

Growing into Iconographic Art

I came to this country from Istanbul, Turkey, in 1974 with only $100 in my pocket. Back home, art had been my love and passion, but here in the United States I had to work during the daytime and go to school at night. After a while the pressure was too much. I felt I had to do something else with my life, so I asked myself, "What made me happy?"

Sketching… I had loved to sketch and work with colors in Istanbul, so I enrolled in the School of Fine Arts in Boston. One of my professors, not an Armenian, worked with church mosaics. He saw my work and suggested I consider iconography.

In Istanbul, I had grown up surrounded by religious art. Every morning before beginning the school day we prayed in the church next door. I remembered looking in awe at the icons. I fell in love with them then. So, years later and miles away from my birthplace, it excited me to think that I might be able to combine my artistic skills with my love for those religious images and produce them myself.

In 1995, I did my first piece and gave it to St. James Armenian Church in Watertown. Then, when Father Arakel became the church pastor, he suggested I do two more pieces for the church. Through my discussions with Father Arakel, I came to realize that, as much as I loved religious images, I really did not know what things meant.

Father Arakel brought religious significance to my work. He explained that, in the Armenian orthodox tradition, when an artist portrays Jesus Christ as a baby, Mary must accompany him and his facial features should be those of a child-man rather than those of a baby, because Jesus, even in infancy, is God. This differs from Catholic iconography in which one often sees the Virgin without child. In the Armenian orthodox tradition Christ is both human and divine, so the baby Jesus must always be with his human mother. Likewise, the stars on the Virgin Mary's forehead and shoulders must be eight-pointed rather than the more common five-pointed. The eight points symbolize wholeness and the second coming of Christ, which is prophesied to occur on the eighth day. I learned a lot from Father Arakel, who also is a painter.

In 2001, I completed the icons for the church, and I am working on others. Through art, I am exploring my personal creativity and religious heritage.

Alice Ashchian-Martin, Watertown, Massachusetts

Healing Dreams

I began to lose my faith in 1979 when my sister, Barbara, was diagnosed with breast cancer. She had one breast removed. Four months later she had her other breast removed. Later, cancer appeared in her lymph nodes and then in her brain. She passed away December 18, 1981, at age thirty-four, leaving behind her husband and ten-year-old daughter.

My sister meant everything to me. She was my best friend. She was a wonderful wife and a great mother to her daughter. Every day she was sick I prayed for God to take me instead of her, because I was single and fewer people depended on me. When she died I could not understand God's plan. I turned away from the church and from God. I stopped dating, too. I was frightened of getting married and having children. I was afraid of getting cancer and leaving young children and my husband like she had.

But after she passed away a curious thing began to happen. One night I had a very bad-feeling dream about her that really disturbed me, but after that one dream I began having wonderful dreams of my sister. I dreamt of us laughing together and of many fun times we had shared over the years. I began to see that the bad dream and the subsequent happy dreams were helping me accept the fact that her life was over. She knew how much I loved children and I felt that the dreams were telling me that she wanted me to move forward and to live my life.

Slowly I began to go out again and I met Stephen, a wonderful Armenian man who was very strong in his Christianity and who had strong family values. He asked me to marry him. I explained that I could not get married and have children even though I loved children and wanted a family more than anything else in the world. We talked about my fears and he convinced me that he was willing to take the chance if I was.

We married, and we regularly attend St. Gregory Armenian Church in Fowler, California. My husband is a deacon in training. I sing in the choir, and our daughters, Barbara (named in memory of my sister) and Samantha, are candle bearers. My lessons were difficult ones, but I learned that life without faith is very lonely and that we should not question or doubt God's plan for us and the people we love.

Judy Krikorian, *Clovis, California*

In the Footsteps of Job

I am an Apostolic Armenian, and I would never change my faith. However, it was a non-Apostolic Christian woman in Armenia who first introduced me to the Holy Bible. She would visit me occasionally, and we would discuss the Bible together. At the end of each visit, she would recommend a chapter for me to read, which I would do upon her departure.

Despite my readings, I could never understand how the Virgin Mary conceived Jesus. After my daughter completed her biological studies, I asked her if there was any instance in the animal world of this happening. My daughter said, "No. There isn't."

Then one day, in 1983, I decided to read the Holy Scripture from the beginning to the end, instead of choosing individual chapters. It was during this period that I reread the episode where Jesus says that only those who think like children will inherit the Kingdom of Heaven. Suddenly, I understood that the miracles and acts of God are beyond human comprehension and that by having approached everything critically I had sinned. I knelt down and asked for God's forgiveness.

Three days later, I received news from Armenia that my daughter had died. I wondered whether my daughter's death had happened so that I could reconsider my approach toward God. No, I realized. God gave her to me. I had enjoyed her for forty years, and now He had chosen to take her away. I consoled myself in this way and grew closer to God.

But that was not the end of it. My thirty-seven-year-old son, Sarkis, and I decided to go to Armenia to visit my daughter's grave and her two children. When the time came to leave for Armenia, I got sick and was unable to get out of bed. I asked my son to change his plans, but he insisted on going, because he had promised to visit my deceased daughter's two children. He went, but shortly after his return, on Labor Day weekend at the seashore, he died of heart attack, nine months after my daughter's death. Again I kneeled down and prayed, "God, You gave him to me and you took him away. Glory to You!"

I lost my second daughter soon after that, too. Today I am left with my fourth and now only son. I thank God every day for His providence, and like a child I have learned to live with his wisdom.

Yeghisabed Sarkisian, *Fowler, California*

Traffic Jam

At about five o'clock one afternoon I was driving home from downtown Chicago, and I hit traffic. The traffic in Chicago is horrendous and that day I just wasn't in the mood to sit in it, so I pulled off the highway at the first exit, thinking that I would rather sit on some side street than sit in traffic.

I pulled over to the side of the road and called the office for my messages. My secretary told me that one of our parishioners had been admitted to the hospital. "Wow," I said. The hospital was one hundred yards from where I was parked.

At the reception desk, I glanced over the roster of patient names for the parishioner and for other Armenian names as well. I noticed one other patient with an Armenian surname, so I asked for her room number too. First I visited with my parishioner. After our visit, I left to find the next Armenian woman's room. Somehow I ended up on the wrong floor and bumped into a third Armenian lady who I had no idea was there. I introduced myself. She told me her husband had died the previous year. We spent some time together talking and praying, and finally I left, determined to find the third patient's room. I did, and, when I entered, she seemed to be sleeping. Suddenly her eyes flew open, and she looked up at me. "What are you doing here?" she asked.

It turned out that she was a member of a parish forty-five minutes north. She had wanted her priest to visit her, but that week he had a terrible cold and since she had had major surgery he could not visit. I don't know how to describe it, other than to say that this woman was just thirsting for a visit from a clergyman.

There's no question in my mind that if it hadn't been for that traffic jam I would never have gotten off the highway at that exit ramp and I never would have seen those three women that day. I don't know how I got there, but I know God sent me to that hospital that day.

Reverend Deacon Aren Jebejian, *Chicago, Illinois*

The Invisible Hand of the Lord

I had major heart surgery in 1998. I am fortunate to be living today. About a year before my surgery, my wife decided to join a health club. I had no intentions of joining myself, but I decided to tag along with her that day, and I got talked into joining the club, too. After joining, I started to really enjoy it. I began to go at least three times a week to walk two or three miles each time on the treadmill.

One day while walking on the treadmill, I began to have a burning sensation in the pit of my stomach. This went on for about a week or two before I mentioned it to one of the club employees. He suggested that I might have a heart problem. I didn't think so, but upon his recommendation and my daughter Terrie's urging I made an appointment to see the doctor.

Prior to my doctor's appointment, we had a bad ice storm. I was heading outside to try and chop up some of the ice when my son Brian said, "Don't go out, Dad. It will melt anyway." Usually I'm pretty stubborn about stuff like that; I like to shovel the snow right away, but for whatever reason, that day I listened to my son and I let the ice melt.

A few days later at the doctor's office, I found out that my major coronary artery was about 90 percent blocked. Two days later, I had open-heart bypass surgery. If I had not joined the health club, or listened to the advice of my son, I would not be alive today. I believe that the Lord was watching over me because he has other plans for me.

Perry Paragamian, *Racine, Wisconsin*

A Tribute to the Memory of the Simsarians

Everybody was killed. Some Armenian legionnaires found me wandering in the fields. They brought me to an orphanage in Suruig, Turkey. Three weeks later, my sister found me. She was able to find me because I have a defining birthmark on my chest.

In 1918, we were transferred to an orphanage in Aleppo, Syria. Armenian papers from America arrived regularly. One day in *Baikar Daily*, published in Watertown, Massachusetts, I saw an advertisement for Dicran Simsarian, Attorney at Law. My sister and I took the ad to the principal of the orphanage, thinking that Dicran might be an uncle of ours. The principal suggested we write a letter. "If he is your uncle he will answer; if not, he won't," the principal said. We never thought it was near impossible that our real uncle had escaped the massacres, gone to America, and become a lawyer. We were too young.

A month later, an answer to our letter arrived. Dicran Simsarian of New Jersey wrote that he was originally from Diarbekir, not the Anatolia region like we were from. We were not related, but he said that we had seen a lot of trouble, and he asked us if we would please accept him as our uncle. He enclosed a $50 check with the letter. He said he would like to have a picture of us. He told us to use the rest of the money for whatever we needed. We began to correspond with him regularly.

In 1922, he wrote us saying that papers were ready for us to come to America. We would live with him. My sister would work during the day and go to school at night, and I would go to public school. On October 1, 1922, we landed in Providence, Rhode Island. He met us at the ship with his attorney. Upon meeting him, my sister said, "You cannot be Dicran Simsarian. You are much too young to do this kind of charitable work."

His attorney said, "I wish everyone had a heart like Dicran."

But it wasn't only him. In New Jersey, we met his wife, Satnig. She was a twenty-two-year-old bride with a six-month-old baby daughter. His mother lived with them, too. Her husband had just started his practice. They had no money. They had borrowed the money to pay for us to come to this country. Don't you think she had a very big heart? She was a very, very nice person. After we came, my sister and I called them Uncle and Aunt. That's the story of how I came to America.

Virgine Kezarjian Mazmanian, *Arlington, Massachusetts*

When I Lost My Mom I Lost My Faith

It was going to be a busy weekend in what was my busy 24-year-old life. I went to school during the day and worked in the evenings, and I was dating the man I planned to marry. That Saturday, my fiancé and I were going to a baby shower. On Sunday, the family was gathering to celebrate my grandparents' fiftieth wedding anniversary. That weekend was my parents' wedding anniversary also.

My mother had been sick with the flu for about three days. She was resting on the couch that morning when I left the house. I promised her I'd pick up some things at the grocery store for the party the next day on our way home from the shower.

That evening, when we returned from the shower, cars were parked everywhere at my parents' home. It was weird. I had no idea what was going on. We were trying to park the car when my father came out of the house. He told us that my mother had suffered a heart attack. The medics had tried to bring her back, but they couldn't save her. She was dead. My mother was dead.

To this day, we don't know if it was heart symptoms that made it look like she had the flu or if it was actually the flu that caused the heart attack. What I do know is that my mother was the foundation of our family, and my two younger sisters and I were completely lost without her.

I could not believe that God would take our mother at such a young age and without any warning. I fell into a severe depression. I was numb. I did not feel love. I didn't feel anything. It was hard to cope with everyday life. It was hard to make it through an entire day. I fell out of love with my husband-to-be. I questioned my faith in God. There were days that I just prayed for God to take my life, too.

Up until then I had been an active member of our church community, so it was natural to talk to Father Kevork. He reminded me that we should not question God or his plan for us. I knew that he was right, but, at the same time, I could not understand why God would take my mother.

I don't remember much about that time. I remember trying to keep busy. I could not handle idle time, because that was when I would start feeling sorry for myself and my depression would really set in. I knew I just had to put my trust in God. I did.

Little by little I became stronger. It took about three months for my feelings to return. I fell in love with my fiancé again. We married as we had planned to before my mother died, and I began attending church regularly again.

In hindsight, I think the key to my spiritual recovery was my husband and I deciding to lead the Armenian Church Youth Organization Youth Leaders group at the church. My mother's death had taught me the importance of living each day to the fullest, because we don't know what tomorrow will bring. I tried to get this message across to the children. The more I gave to these children, the more they gave back to me and the stronger my faith became. My husband and I have led our youth group for fifteen years now, and each year of working with the kids brings me the same wonderful rewards.

My first child was born on the anniversary of my mother's death four years later. I don't believe that is a coincidence. I think God knew how painful that day was for me so he gave me my child on that day. Then, even more ironically, four years after my first child was born, my father died the exact same way my mother had on the exact same weekend. Part of me could not believe that God had done this to me and our family again. I did not lose my faith the second time, but I slipped a little bit.

Our lives are in God's hands. He has the plan. He has the control. What we can do is to pray and trust Him. I learned that from these experiences. I learned to live each minute of every day as if it were my last, and I learned that the best way to do this is to give to others. The more you give, the more you receive, and the stronger your faith becomes.

Laurie Nalbandian, *Fowler, California*

Answered Prayers

I believe in prayer.

After my brother passed away, and my father and my grandmother, only my Mom and I were left. I had long before been diagnosed with a progressive disabling disease. My mother was my primary care giver and companion as well as my mother and only family.

Then she got sick. It was her heart. She spent the last year of her life in and out of the hospital. The last time she went in, it was just to recheck her medicine and make sure her heart was doing what it was supposed to do. When I arrived home after visiting her one afternoon, the phone was ringing. It was the doctor. She had fallen into a coma.

I rushed back to the hospital to find my mother attached to all sorts of life-support equipment. The doctor told me that if she responded right away, that would be a good sign. The longer she didn't respond, the worse the possible outcome. She could end up like a vegetable.

There was nothing I could do, so I went downstairs to the hospital chapel. That's where my Mom used to go to pray for me when I was in the same hospital facing the same life-or-death balance. I sat in the chapel for a while feeling as alone as I was. Finally, I said, "You know Lord, I really don't know how to pray. All I know is that my mother came here and prayed for me when I was sick and that you answered her prayers." I told Him that I loved my mother and that more than anything I wanted her to live, but I knew too that it might not be fair to her. If she was not going to live and have a pretty normal life, I asked Him to please take her right away and not let her linger. I said thank you, sat awhile longer, and left.

A few hours later my mother passed on. "Did you remove the machines? I asked. The doctor said no, she went on her own.

God had answered my prayer.

Rose Zinakorjian, *Chicago, Illinois*

The Hand of God

What has become clear to me as I get older is how the hand of God has been in my life *in spite of* the decisions I've made. There are certain times when you arrive at a place and look back, and in looking back you realize that you've come to that place quite in spite of your willful disregard of certain things—in spite of your stupidity or laziness or negligence. And nevertheless, through all of those things, God's will for you has not been thwarted.

When I proposed to my wife, I wanted it to be at a place that would be eternal. In New York City it's hard to find eternal things, but I thought of the Statue of Liberty. Hopefully it will be around for the duration of my lifetime, and certainly if it were ever destroyed something terrible would have happened.

It was a cold, blustery day, but there was a moment of brightness as I was down on my knee asking her to marry me. I gave her my grandmother's engagement ring. As I did, I felt that the eyes of the generations were looking down on me and viewing this moment as a point in the whole family lineage. Its future was taking shape right there; our family's life was moving forward and taking a certain path. I recalled that I met my wife as a result of a strange coincidence we still laugh over. Then it occurred to me that I had not really chosen to walk along this path. I had come upon it partially through luck, partially through blessedness, but somehow as much through my indecision as through my active decision. And in both cases, I felt, I had been guided towards this blessed moment—without realizing it, of course, except in retrospect at the moment of fruition.

If every day in your marriage demonstrates in some small way that you were guided towards it by a greater force—a force greater than yourself, greater than either one of you—it's a wonderful situation to live in.

Christopher Zakian, *New York, New York*

A Personal Experience with Angels

On September 12, 1994, I had a heart attack. I did not accept what was happening until my husband came home from the coffee shop and said, "Marilyn, why are you home and not at work?"

The paramedics came and took me to the hospital. They tried to do an angiogram but couldn't. They said I was too far gone. The first doctor gave us no hope at all. But my children got on the phone and called another doctor who called another doctor who was in Visalia visiting friends. That doctor said that he would do the surgery if he could. After he arrived and evaluated me, he told my kids that I would be fine. My kids came in and told me the news. They were crying. I said, "Don't worry. The Good Lord is with me. I know He is with me."

My recovery from surgery took twice as long as what was considered normal. I was on a respirator for days rather than hours. While I was on the respirator, three ladies came and stood beside me. They asked if they could watch and said they would take care of me. I thought they were nurses because they were dressed in white. The next thing I remember was a Hindu-looking man standing over me. I said, "I'm cold. So cold." The ladies kept saying, "You're all right, honey. You're all right." The Hindu put a sheet over my head and began washing my body like they did in the olden times before they buried you. I said, "They are washing my body. I've died. I've died!"

Outside my room, I heard crying and people saying, "Poor Marilyn, she shouldn't have gone like this." And I remember my sister coming into the room. I remember her because she had a red blouse on. Later I asked her if she did have a red blouse on and she said yes. She told me that she had come to tell me I was doing great and to have faith.

Then I remember bells ringing like they do in the church. The whole time I kept saying, "Oh, I've died. What are my kids going to do? What is my husband going to do?" The next thing I remember is Father Kevork standing over me saying the Lord's Prayer. "Der Hayr, did I die?" I asked him. "No," he said. " You are fine. The Lord is with you."

After my recovery I told the doctor about the three ladies and the Hindu man. The doctor said I must have been hallucinating, but I don't think I was. I believe there are angels and that angels were looking over me.

Since then my whole attitude about life has changed. I know where my priorities are, whereas I didn't really know before that experience. I've become more loving and more understanding and more caring. I never used to pray. Now I pray maybe ten times a day. I read my Bible when I never used to. I haven't missed a day of church except a few Sundays when we were out of the country on vacation. I go even if I'm not feeling well. If I'm not feeling well, I go, and, while I'm there, I perk up and I'm great.

Marilyn L. Pattigan, *Parlier, California*

Defying the Odds

A woman in my parish was a single parent. It was just her and her thirteen-year-old son. I was at the hospital with her when she had surgery. After the operation, the doctors told her that she had cancer. They gave her three months to live and told her to expect to be bedridden and catheterized the whole time. When the doctors left, she looked up at me and said, "They're wrong." She was determined that her son would not lose his mother before he could take care of himself. She vowed to live long enough to see him independent. I encouraged her, and we prayed.

One Sunday, about two months later, she and her son came to church. That itself was amazing because, according to the doctors, she was supposed to have never gotten out of bed again. Then, at communion time, she came up to receive Holy Communion on her own power. You could have sliced the silence in the congregation with a knife as everybody watched her slow yet deliberate walk to where I stood at the front of the sanctuary.

Her message was clear: The doctors are wrong. I'm going to live!

Well, she did. She lived another six or seven years or more. She drove a car again, and she went back to work. As time passed, she got around so normally you would never know how ill she had been, and still was. Her son was an independent, young adult, attending college and working when she passed away.

She placed herself totally in God's hands, and, combined with her own determination, she defied the medical establishment and overcame all kinds of odds. As her priest, I can tell you that it wasn't easy. Her triumph was a real faith lesson for everybody in the parish.

Reverend Father Vartan Kasparian, *Visalia, California*

The Power of Prayer

Not too long ago, a group of women friends, seven in all, felt that time was passing by and we were not seeing one another enough, so we decided to meet periodically for lunch at various local restaurants. At one such occasion, one of the women invited a guest. To my delight, her guest was an old childhood friend of mine whom I had not seen in years. Julie and I had grown up in the same neighborhood. We were both Armenian and had played together often as kids. Our lives had taken different paths, but we had never forgotten each other.

Julie and I agreed that we had a lot of catching up to do, so a few weeks later, I called to see if she could get together again, just the two of us. To my surprise, when I called, she was unable to come to the phone. Her husband said that she was having health problems and was preparing to go into the hospital. I was shocked—only a short time before she had sat across from me at lunch, bubbling and energetic.

When I called back to see how things were going there was no answer, so I left a message. Julie returned my call some weeks later. It was tiring and difficult for her to talk but she wanted me to know how much my calls and concern meant to her. Then she told me that someone had listed her name in the church bulletin as someone who was ill and in need of prayers. Because people knew she was sick, a flood of calls, cards, and prayers had been pouring in from members of the Armenian community. "People are so kind," she said. "I'd really like to thank the person who thought to put my name in the bulletin. It wasn't you was it, Gloria?"

"It was," I admitted with a sigh of relief. After placing her name in the bulletin, it had occurred to me that maybe she didn't want people to know she was sick and that I should have asked for her permission before doing it.

We talked for a long time that day. Her illness was serious, and the doctors had not paved an easy road ahead. Before hanging up, she thanked me again for letting the community know that she was sick and for asking them for their prayers and support.

Over the next months, Julie and I continued to keep in touch. We spoke often of God's goodness and of the power of prayer and positive thinking. Thanks to our pastor, Julie's name stayed in the church bulletin and she continued to receive prayers from our parishioners.

Then one day my phone rang. It was Julie. She was excited and happy. "It's a miracle," she said. To the amazement of all her doctors, her condition had changed. Her illness was still serious, but far from what they originally thought. She would have to be checked routinely, and she might need further therapy, but of a less drastic nature. Her improvement was indeed a miracle.

I believe in the power of prayer. I believe that, if you surround yourself with loving people, think good thoughts, hold steadfast in your faith, and trust in the power of prayer, miracles can and do happen. They did for my dear friend, Julie.

Gloria Semonian, *Royal Oak, Michigan*

Nowhere to Take Her

On January 13, 1999, my daughter and her girlfriend were driving back to school at four o'clock in the afternoon for a cheerleading meeting when a truck swerved across the median and killed them both instantly. I was on my way to Sacramento. One of my friends, an Armenian businessman in Fowler, called me on my cell phone. He tried to get me to turn around without upsetting me too much or really telling me that my seventeen-year-old daughter was dead, but I knew in my heart that she was.

As I drove back to Fowler, I realized that because my wife and I were both non-practicing Catholics I had not formed any relationships with a religious community. Now, my daughter was dead, and I had no place to take her.

The first person to meet me at my house was Father Kevork, pastor of St. Gregory's, the Armenian Church in town. Father Kevork was a big reason I kept my sanity. I am a reactive individual, and my first thought was to take revenge. He calmed me down and stayed by our side all through the ordeal. He explained to me that there is an afterlife and that my daughter was in a better place. He told me over and over that God had his reasons for taking her. It's still tough for me to understand that, but I'm trying.

From then on we joined the Armenian Apostolic Church. It was an easy transition for us. Over the years, even without my guidance, my daughter had sought out her own religious experience. She had attended both the Presbyterian Church and St. Gregory's, but she had favored St. Gregory's because of her friendship with Father Kevork's son and because of the many girlfriends she had who attended there. In the town of Fowler, there are many Armenians. Growing up, all my buddies were Armenians, and many of my wife's friends too. Today, our two younger children attend Armenian Sunday School, and I barbeque at the events with a bunch of the guys. We have found a spiritual home and community at St. Gregory's.

I learned that it is important to give your children some background about God and his teachings that they can then develop into their own religious experience as they mature. My daughter was a senior in high school, a cheerleader, president of this and that—all that good stuff—and, as her father, as the head of my family, I had no place to take her when she died. It was a bad feeling I had. I don't ever want to have that feeling again.

Michael Martin, *Fowler, California*

Life Choices

My career moves have definitely been affected by my faith, and particularly by the location of Armenian churches. I was born and raised in Lowell, Massachusetts. I went to Sunday School and served on the altar at Sts. Vartanantz. In 1973, when I graduated with a degree in chemistry, I had many job opportunities all over the United States, but I took a job in Syracuse, New York, because there are two Armenian churches there. While in Syracuse, I received a tremendous offer to manage a state-of-the-art laboratory in a newly constructed pharmaceutical plant located in McPherson, Kansas. It was a very prestigious position, but I refused it because there wasn't an Armenian church within 500 miles.

When it comes to my Armenian Christian heritage, I'm not afraid to say that in a way I'm like a baby attached by an umbilical cord to his mother's womb. Living near an Armenian church has been essential to me. I believe I would have withered away had I lived without contact with my church and community.

The types of companies I've worked for also are a testimony to my faith. I could not work for a tobacco company or an arms company. It would just be against my moral fiber. I've tried to work for companies that would benefit mankind. I've worked for pharmaceutical and energy-related companies, and currently I'm working in the area of construction materials.

Ara Jeknavorian, *Chelmsford, Massachusetts*

A Holy Thursday Healing

My immediate family and most of my extended family are devoted Christians. We do not need to experience miracles to believe as we do; we rely on faith. There is, however, one instance that happened to my Dad which reinforced for us that God does indeed work miracles.

Heidi Kadamian, *Racine, Wisconsin*

* * *

In 1965, when I was ten years old, I was serving as an acolyte at St. Mesrob Armenian Church in Racine. It was Holy Week. Our priest, Father Dajad Davidian, called the house on Monday to ask my mother if my brother and I could have our feet washed at the service on Holy Thursday. My mother said that my brother could have his feet washed, but she explained that since November of the year before I'd had a bad fungus on my right foot. After numerous trips to the doctor and many prescribed medicines, we still had not found a cure. In fact, the fungus was worse than ever. My foot was varying shades of purple and green, and wearing socks and shoes was painful. Father Dajad said that he would still like to wash my feet but would do mine last.

On Holy Thursday, my feet were washed after all the others. Then Father Dajad marked the sign of the cross on my injured foot with butter. I honestly didn't think anything of it at the time. Having your feet washed on Holy Thursday was an honor, but nothing really out of the ordinary.

That night before bed my mother told me not to put any medicine on, to just leave my foot alone for a night. So that's what I did. The next morning when I woke, the fungus was completely gone. I can't explain what happened to me except to say that our Lord can and does work miracles.

George Kadamian, *Racine, Wisconsin*

Focal Points of Peace

I work in a large medical laboratory. In my little corner of the office where I have my desk and all my belongings, I have a few angel figurines that friends have given to me as gifts. My "What would Jesus do?" bracelet hangs around the neck of one of them. Posted above my desk is my favorite Lenten phrase from the Peace Hour Service, *Zee Asdvadz unt mez eh* (For God is with us).

First thing every morning, I pause to look at these things for just a moment and think about what the day is going to bring and how I might best approach it. No matter how difficult a day gets, I know I can go to my desk and find my little focal point of peace. It sure makes the job easier.

Lauren Chalekian, *Racine, Wisconsin*

Regular Maintenance

Christianity is about regular maintenance. Living a Christian life is like changing the oil in a car. You can change your oil every 3000 miles as the book recommends, and your car will run for a long time. You can change your oil every 2500 miles instead of every 3000 miles, and your car will probably run even better. Or you cannot change your oil at all. At some point your car will just stop running, and it's likely that it will stop running a lot earlier than it would have had you been doing regular maintenance.

I don't need to have my faith tested when I need it most. That's the mistake. The mistake is ignoring your faith until something really horrible happens. That's not the way you live a Christian life. You live a Christian life when you miss the bus, your college application is rejected, someone doesn't show up for a meeting, or you throw a party and no one comes. Every day, every minute, involves looking at life as a Christian. Recognizing those little tests of faith is what I call regular maintenance.

Charlie Shooshan, *Newington, Connecticut*

Francine

When Tom and I were first married, we were sure that we would have a brood of children. Then we had difficulty conceiving. We went through fertility testing. We went through the frustration, the fears, and the miscarriages. Nothing worked. It was difficult to accept that God's plan for us meant we could not have children of our own, but we finally had to acknowledge that this was the way it was going to be.

Originally I was much more interested in adoption than Tom was. So we started investigating the options slowly. We had been married ten years before we found ourselves actively seeking adoption. Maybe it took that long for us to open our hearts?

There are many ways to adopt. Counseling sessions with Father Kevork helped us sort through our options and find the right one for us as a family. We discovered that, because of our faith, our path to adoption was very narrow. Everything had to be open and aboveboard. We did not want money to change hands.

We decided to pursue what's called an open adoption, meaning that the birth parents select their child's adoptive parents. This process requires a lot of honest self-evaluation. We had to put together an autobiographical book for the birth moms to look at and select from. Our book contained photographs and stories from both of our lives. Everything that had happened to us, good or bad, went into our presentation.

One of the things we worried about was that we clearly stated that we were going to raise our adopted child in the Armenian Orthodox Church. If you are not in the Armenian community, "Armenian" sounds foreign, and the word "orthodox" scares a lot of people. But we made the choice to include it in our book, because it is who we are.

Interestingly, it turned out not to be an issue for the birth mother who selected us. To me it is an example of how we have to do what we think is right. The right thing may seem difficult at the time, but it has to be done. For us, stating our intent to raise our child as an Armenian Christian was a lesson in humility and honesty. After all, adopting a child is at the very base of human relationships.

The waiting period in the adoption process is a time when you really have to put your faith in God. The truth is, if it is going to happen it will, and if it isn't it won't. After months of waiting, and out of who we truly are and how we are shaped, we were blessed with a wonderful little girl named

Francine. Neither Tom nor I can imagine life without her. Had we been able to have our own children, we would have missed out on knowing her. Now I can look back at all we went through and truly say that not having the opportunity to know Francine would have been sad.

Tom and I often look at each other and crack up laughing because we find Francine far more interesting that anything we would have produced genetically. Being blond haired and blue eyed, Francine stands out in the Armenian community, but everyone includes her as one of the family.

Linda Miles, *Fresno, California*

Do You Believe in God?

When I went to Armenia for the first time in February of 1992, I went as an employee of the Armenian Church of America. The fellow who drove us around was a big Iranian-looking Armenian: black hair, red skin, a striking fellow. With his Eastern Armenian and my bad Western Armenian, we were able to chat and have simple conversations. Over the days, we got good at it. At one point during some down-time, we were chatting and he asked, "Chris, do you believe in God?"

Immediately, I began to answer the question in a roundabout way: "Well, I work for the church… it's an important institution…blah, blah, blah." Then in mid-sentence I stopped speaking. It suddenly occurred to me that I was not answering this man's question. I looked at him and said, "Yes. I do believe in God."

Afterward, I recalled this experience, because I was wondering what it was that had made me, just as a matter of habit, hesitate in answering his question in the most obvious and forthright way. I don't know exactly what it was, but in part I think it had to do with some sort of embarrassment, that this was not the type of question a sophisticated person gave a simple yes-or-no answer to. It had to be qualified and intellectualized somehow.

But this fellow, obviously wrongly assuming that I was a sophisticated and wise and intelligent person, was asking me if I believed in God. At first, I had been unwilling to be straightforward with him. Thankfully, I was able to give him the direct answer that he deserved. That *all* Armenians deserve.

Christopher Zakian, *New York, New York*

The Potato Crop

When I was living in Armenia, I decided I wanted to help my neighbors plant potatoes in their field near my house. When I told them I wanted to help, they laughed at me. They said the work of planting was too hard for me. Their doubts made me insistent. I wanted to show them. I planted potatoes for a few hours before I could not bend over any longer because my back hurt so much. I got a taste for how hard their work really was. I stopped, but they continued to work for many more weeks doing all the things you have to do to cultivate a crop of potatoes.

Then a month or so later, I was visiting my neighbors when right before dinner everyone rushed to the window. Huge hail stones were falling from the sky. Hail is not good for crops. The storm decimated half of the potato crop in minutes. I was beside myself. I thought about all that work I did, they did, and how it was gone.

My neighbor was upset, but his overriding emotion seemed to be acceptance. He shrugged and spoke about things just happening and about how nothing is really yours and how you should not take anything for granted. People who live tied to the earth and who are poor in material things, like many people in Armenia, seem to have a resignation about life that we tend to forget by having too much here in the United States. I learned a lot about faith from helping plant that field of potatoes in Armenia. I learned that, whatever God gives you, be grateful for, and, whatever he takes, well, it was not yours in the first place.

Jason Demerjian, *Waltham, Massachusetts*

I Wept

One summer in the early 1980s, I traveled in Armenia for a couple of weeks with my family and some Armenian friends. Of course, one of the visits we made was to the mother church at Etchmiadzin. It was Sunday morning, and there was a service going on in the church. I remember walking into the sanctuary with my family and standing, because there are no pews in the church at Etchmiadzin.

As I stood in this ancient and beautiful church, I began to scan the faces of the Armenians who had come to worship that day. Most of them were wonderfully intent on the service. Many held their arms outstretched before them as if they were receiving the spirit of Jesus Christ right there in that particular place at that particular moment. Then I noticed a few people lying down, sort of kneeling down, and putting their entire body onto the floor in front of God. It was as if they were giving their entire lives, their beings, and their souls to Him. I was so moved by my fellow worshipers and the entire atmosphere of the *Badarak*—the smell of the incense burning, the flickering candles—and by just being in that ancient Armenian place of worship that I began to sob. Worshiping with people so dedicated to spirituality and faith meant something to me that I could not describe in words. The only thing I could do was cry.

After that experience, I regained my composure, and we had lunch with a priest who was also a dear family friend, so it was a very nice afternoon.

Seta Nersessian, *Westwood, Massachusetts*

Pride

There is no need to draw undo attention to oneself. That's a key ingredient of living Christian faith. We speak about pride as one of the major sins. Pride is a tough one because you want to feel good about yourself; you want to feel that it is good to be a Christian; you want to have self-respect and self-esteem. How can it be possible that pride is a deadly sin?

I think the answer is when your goal is to be better than others. Not just to be considered one of God's creatures, but to want a front row seat in Heaven—that's what the deadly sin of pride is about.

In my first year of teaching at a public high school in Connecticut, I had a student in one of my classes who was among the tallest, handsomest, most athletic, and most popular students in school. One day, this particular student, while sitting in class, started choking. Since he was very large and obviously perceived as very strong, none of the students in class believed that this was something serious. They thought he was kidding or he had a weird cough or something. I immediately recognized that he literally wasn't able to breathe. I jumped up and had to practically stand on a chair to perform the Heimlich maneuver on him because he was so tall. Something shot out of his mouth, and as luck would have it, I caught it in my hand. He started to breathe again. We went into the hallway, walked around, and talked a little bit. Ten minutes later we were back in class.

It turned out that, on a whim, as teenagers might, he had purchased an artificial cap that fit over a real tooth to make it look like he had a gold tooth. In class, this non-functional, decorative piece of gold had somehow popped off his tooth, lodged in his throat, and threatened his life. Without exaggeration, he almost died choking on a fake gold tooth.

For me that was the end of the story, and it would have been the end of the story had I not been approached the following day by a school administrator who had heard about what happened. He explained that the school often did not get enough good press in the community. He suggested we call a reporter from the local newspaper to take a picture of me and the student and to write a nice article about the Heimlich maneuver and how I had used it to save this student's life. "It will make the student look good, it will make you look good, and it will improve the impression in the community of the school," he said.

This is the part of the story where the Christian faith put its stamp. Up to then I had acted according to the basic rules of humanity. Someone needed my assistance in class, and I gave him assistance. That is living on autopilot. That is being good people. It was the next day, when my administrator spoke with me, that I had to dig down and respond in a way that was not a knee-jerk reaction.

"No. We are not going to do that," I said. "This student is one of the most popular students in school. He is on the football team. He has a lot of good feelings about himself. Others respect him. I don't think it would serve him to have his picture in the paper standing next to a teacher who saved his life. I don't care how good it will make me look or the school look, ultimately it will embarrass him, and I don't want to do that." Thankfully, I have some very warm and caring administrators. They immediately adopted my position, and the issue was dropped.

Then somehow the student found out what I had done. I didn't intend for him to find out, but he found out, and he thanked me for not putting him through the embarrassment of having to be the person saved in the fire, so to speak. Ultimately, a whole bunch of people began to be very friendly to me after that because on his own terms and in his own way he told the people he wanted to know what I had done and they in turn said, "Hey that Mr. Shooshan, he's a pretty good guy."

Had I decided to use the event to get my picture in the paper and show all my family and friends how I saved this kid's life, the benefit of living in my faith would never have come to me. I may have felt a false sense of pride that I did something good, because people would say, "Hey I saw that article about you in the paper. You sure did a good thing. What a good person you are." But they would not really care, because they were not there. They were not the people who were involved in what had happened. By putting the student and his feelings first, I actually got a real benefit rather than a perceived benefit from what happened that day in my classroom, and that's the difference.

Charlie Shooshan, *Newington, Connecticut*

My First Job in Forty-Three Years

This is the first year I have worked outside the home in forty-three years. After loosing my sister to cancer, I moved from Racine, Wisconsin, to Chicago to be closer to my children. My daughter got me a job confirming appointments at a large beauty salon in the area. Over 175 girls, ranging in age from twenty to twenty-six years old, work at the salon. That's a lot of young girls in one room.

For the first few months, I was very quiet. Basically, I listened and watched the girls interact with each other and their clients. Kids are just so different today. I never realized just how different because I was only really involved with my own family and my own children. Many of the girls have multiple sets of parents—a mother here, a stepfather there. Most are out on their own and live from paycheck to paycheck. I have never been in contact with younger people like I have been this past year, and I had not realized how much heartbreak and unhappiness there is out there.

Soon I began to think about how I might be able to help some of the girls. I started by making a few comments. I thought I might make a few of the girls angry with me, but that was not the case. As the months passed, I noticed that they began to approach me with their problems. I listen to them, and I try to help them by suggesting solutions based on what is right and what is wrong according to God's teachings—according to the way I have been taught. They don't get advice from their own mothers, and they don't have to take my advice, but there have been many times when I've received quiet thanks a few days later for listening to them, and they tell me how much better they feel about the situation or problem they are facing.

That's how I help. I get a lot of respect from them. Respect that I don't see them give their peers. It upsets me to see how they treat each other. Too often I have to turn around and look at them. They know I'm disgusted at the language that they are using and how they are treating other people. But I've noticed that in general they are calming down. They are beginning to speak more nicely to one another.

Every night before I go to bed I think about the people I've been in contact with that day. I think about what a young girl had talked to me about, and I pray that I can help at least one person tomorrow. I thank God every night for my job. I love it so much I would do it without pay.

Mary Stevoff, *Chicago, Illinois*

A Long Struggle with Divorce

I married an Armenian man who was a member of our church. He was twelve years older than I. He was well educated and had a secure job. My mother approved of him. He seemed to embody all the things Armenian parents think are right for their children. But it didn't work out. Twenty-six years of marriage and three children later, my husband told me that he did not want to be married. I realized that he was a man who should never have gotten married.

I am a person of strong beliefs, and I truly believe that marriage is for life. When I got divorced I felt like I had failed. I felt that somehow I had wronged God. I struggled with those feelings for a long, long time, and I still struggle with them.

In those early years after the breakup of my marriage, I felt I could not go to the Armenian Church because I was a divorced woman. Even though none of the pastors made me feel that because I was divorced I was not a good person, I was not so sure our community was as tolerant on some things as it should be. The divorce forced me to reach out to people outside my immediate family, church, and community—something I had been reluctant to do before, and may never have done had my marriage remained intact. It took me awhile before I returned to the Armenian Church, but I did return.

Today, I am able to look back and see that, as a result of the divorce, I grew in a different direction as a person than I would have had my marriage survived. Given my issues with the failure of my marriage, I never felt that dating or remarrying were options for me. I chose to remain single, and now I think God may have meant for me to be by myself. It may not make sense to some people, but I believe I am exactly where God has intended for me to be. It is not where I would have liked to be, but it is where I am. I still wish I wasn't divorced. I will always wish I wasn't divorced, but I am learning to accept it.

Gloria Semonian, *Royal Oak, Michigan*

Talking to God

As Sunday School Superintendent I like to drop in on the various classes once in a while to observe what they are doing. One morning I dropped into the preschool class. The teacher had the kids talking to God using toy telephones. I sat down and began to listen. A couple of the children were carrying on the sweetest conversations, saying things like, "Please, God, take care of my grandma because she's sick," or "Look after my brother because he has a broken leg."

In the midst of all these conversations, one little girl picked up her phone, listened for a second, and said in a loud voice, "There's nobody there."

That's kind of how it is, isn't it? Our job is to help our children make sure that they know God answers the other end of line.

Lauren Chalekian, *Racine, Wisconsin*

No Guarantees

One day a few years back, a young lady I knew well went shopping at the mall. In the parking garage, she was kidnapped, beaten, and shot to death. Some nutcase killed her for no reason. How could God allow this to happen? Especially to her? She had been studying and preparing to go abroad to help others by doing relief and development work.

I could not see any good coming out of this senseless act of impersonal violence. My faith flipped upside down.

The Armenian song, *"Oor Eyir Asdvadz"* ("Where were you God?") played over and over in my mind. Let's face it. The issue of the Genocide is a tough stumbling block for all of us Armenians. Many Armenians ask themselves, "Where was God when the massacres were going on?" I asked myself the same questions. "Where was God when my friend was at the mall? Why would something like this happen?"

Someone recommended I read a book called *The Apostolic Fathers*. The book is not about the Disciples of Christ but about the lives of the early church leaders who were the disciples of the Disciples. I discovered that every one of the early Christian leaders suffered severe persecution. Persecution that often led to death.

Suddenly, I realized that there are no guarantees. There are no guarantees that as Christians we will have an easy life, that everything will go our way, or that our businesses will be successful.

Just as suddenly, the answer to my questions came to me.

As Christians we do have a guarantee that God will go through those struggles with us. Each of those early church leaders felt God by their side in the middle of their persecution. His presence gave them the strength to endure.

My faith changed that day. I no longer expect that because I am a Christian everything will go well for me. Because of what happened to my friend, my faith now says, "Whatever I go through, I know that God is going to go through it with me and that He will give me the strength to go through whatever life dishes out."

We went through hell as a nation, but today most of us are not suffering. We live in a culture and in a country that are very prosperous. We have good families and we tend to be successful. But we suffered, and because we as Armenians were the first to suffer Genocide in the last century, I believe that our task today, as a people and as a church, is to be the first to speak out against and to help those who are suffering today—Armenian or non-Armenian.

Richard Melikian, *Phoenix, Arizona*

Heritage

A Piece of the Puzzle

When I deal with other Christians around the world, I feel that Armenian Apostolic Christians have this rich legacy that we have sort of kept to ourselves. Other Christians are always interested in knowing about this first Christian nation. They want to know how we developed our unique witness to Christ starting from Thaddaeus and Bartholomew and continuing almost 2000 years to the present. Historic Armenia is a country that lays claim to Noah's Ark, and, at the site of Etchmiadzin, our Holy See, in 301 A.D., Christ came down in a vision to St. Gregory. There are only a few places in the world where that has happened.

For people who really do believe in Christ, I think Armenia carries part of the mystery. There's an allure—sort of like a Christian Tibet. I'm not saying that we necessarily live up to that, but, for people seeking to understand Christianity better, I believe our church and our traditions and our religious sites offer a lot of answers. We are part of the greater Christian puzzle. And we are a part of the puzzle that very few people understand. I am not sure even we understand how valuable our piece of the puzzle is.

Although we're not a proselytizing church, a part of faith and of one's spiritual growth is getting to the point where you understand yourself and your relations with God well enough to talk about it with other people. I think it's also part of how we should relate to other Christians and the rest of the world community.

At the parish I attend regularly in Armenia, we have been holding catechism-type, question-and-answer sessions as a part of our religious education program. One of the issues we discussed recently was our Christian calling. As Christians we are asked to be the salt of the earth, the light, and the yeast of the bread—the leaven and lump. When I talk about the leaven and lump, one of the things I always emphasize is that each Christian, as they come to better understand the faith and their role in it, has a duty to explain it to others. That is how the lump becomes leaven; how the yeast raises the world.

I think this calling is an aspect of our faith that many Armenian Christians don't take seriously or haven't taken the time to understand well enough. I think that, if we tried passing our understanding of Christianity along to others, we might discover a great truth: By your students you will be taught.

That has certainly been my experience. I've discovered time and time again that, in trying to learn something well enough to teach someone else, even if you don't learn it well enough, just the act of trying gives you insight, helps you grow, and helps them grow as well.

Teaching others is at the core of Christianity. It's the basic message, the great commission. Not just the apostles were given the task of spreading the good news. It was given to them and to everyone else. Thaddeus and Bartholomew passed their mission on to us and that commission continues to this day. We are an important part of that commission, and I think we have carried that on within our own community. It is time we reach out to other communities as well. Not necessarily to proselytize and bring them into the Armenian Apostolic faith, but to let people know that in over 2000 years we have come to understand God and Christianity not just by learning and teaching the faith, but also by living it through our history.

I want to share the lessons we have learned with the rest of the world. One way I see of sharing our unique witness is by being empathetic with people who are being oppressed, by being voices for justice or voices against injustice, and by trying to be peacemakers. We have experienced all these things as a nation, so I have found it very easy to work in the area of human rights and for organizations like Amnesty International, because as an Armenian it is as if you are raised with a sense of injustice and the need to champion the causes of the oppressed.

I think that we have that kind of empathy if we want to tap into it, but oftentimes we don't. We become inward-looking, and we see ourselves as victims, but that victimization is also a source of strength. We need to turn those feelings around because in doing so we will show others, and ourselves, that we are able to overcome the injustices we have faced.

Miraculously, for 2000 years we have overcome a great deal of adversity. I think this is largely because we have a faith that gives us hope that things will get better—not only that things will get better but that we have a duty to make them better.

Tom Samuelian, *Yerevan, Armenia*

Witness

When King Drtad picked Christianity as the Armenian national religion in 301, he picked the wrong horse and we have paid for it dearly—over and over and over and over. Think about it. During how much of our history have we been surrounded by foreign enemies trying to cram their religions down our throats? At some point, the critical mass of Armenians could have said, "To hell with this. This is not making a lot of sense." But we stuck with Jesus Christ.

Our continuous faith is witness to the world that Jesus Christ is real. We have always had a choice, and we have always chosen Christ. Our Christianity became not only a means for us to survive, but, whether we realized it or not, it became a reason for us to survive.

Reverend Father Yeprem Kelegian, *Racine, Wisconsin*

Conversion Was an Option

My father told me that we as Armenians had the option of not going through what we went through during the massacres—if we denounced our faith. That's something our people could not do. All of our ancestors, at great personal cost, passed on a heritage and a faith to us. We have to be very careful what we do with it.

Where would we be today had our ancestors converted to Islam?

Richard Hagopian, *Visalia, California*

Bringing the Flame of St. Gregory to Cleveland

To kick off the 1700th Anniversary celebration of our nation's conversion to Christianity, His Holiness Karekin II brought the burning flame of St. Gregory the Illuminator out of the dark pit at Khorvirab in Armenia to Etchmiadzin, our Holy See, where His Holiness then passed it to each Armenian bishop from around the world and to the President of the Republic of Armenia. After receiving the flame, our Primate, Archbishop Khajag Barsamian, then carried the light halfway across the world to the Cathedral in New York City. Two young adults from each parish in the Diocese were invited to receive the light of St. Gregory on behalf of their parishes from the Primate at the Christmas morning service at the Cathedral. At the service, the Primate planned to light a lantern for each parish with the flame he had brought from Armenia. The light of the Illuminator was then to be taken back to each parish and placed on the altar where it would burn throughout the year of celebration.

At St. Gregory of Narek Armenian Church in Cleveland, we were excited about participating in this historic event. We selected a young man and a young woman to go to New York and represent our parish. But figuring out how to bring the flame from New York to Cleveland without it going out became a struggle. For some, the desire to keep the flame burning continuously in our church's lantern once it was received by our youth representatives may seem like a technicality, but the idea that the flame would be put out after the Patriarch had made special provisions for it to burn all the way from Armenia did not sit well with me. Realizing that the lanterns would need to be put out after our youth representatives received the flame, the Patriarch announced that after Christmas two students from St. Nersess Seminary would drive the flame around the country and relight the lanterns. That was an option for our parish, but it still meant that our lantern would have to be put out in New York and lit again in Cleveland. Since flying the flame on an airplane without special permission was out of the question, it became clear to me that the only way to get the original flame from the pit of St. Gregory in Armenia to Ohio was to drive it by car.

As the holidays approached, the travel plans of the people involved got even more confusing. Rather than sorting themselves out, I found out that, due to scheduling difficulties, it would help the St. Nersess students who were driving the flame around the country if we could drive our flame back from New York. But the young woman representing our parish at the service ended up needing to be back in Chicago for school, so she decided it was best for her to fly. The young man agreed to drive with me to New York, but a few days before Christmas he came down with a bad cold, and he too decided to fly.

I was left to decide whether I should let our two youth emissaries go to New York alone and have the seminarians drive the flame to Cleveland, or if I should drive to New York alone in order to drive the flame back to Cleveland. On one hand, I wanted to experience receiving the light of St. Gregory in person and I wanted to be with our two youth representatives at the service, but to go to New York meant having to leave my wife and two kids at Christmas time as well as not being there for my parish to do Christmas services.

Finally, I realized that I just had to stop and ask God what to do. As soon as I let go of the situation and listened, the solution came to me. In Eastern orthodoxy, the spirit moves through our hearts, and my heart was directing me to participate in the service and bring the flame of St. Gregory back to my parish in Cleveland. I knew at once that it was the right decision.

On Friday afternoon, January 5, I hit the road for New York City. It was snowing, and it had been snowing all day. Hours later, the visibility and the driving conditions were so bad on the dark, windy, snow-covered mountainous roads outside of Philadelphia that I had to follow the rear lights of a truck much of the way. It was a long, stressful ride, but I played Christmas music the entire way, and I enjoyed every minute of that.

I arrived in Manhattan before midnight, and I was at the Cathedral by 8:30 the next morning. The doors were open, but no one was there yet. The Cathedral is inspiring in and of itself, but that morning—decorated with a twenty-foot-tall Christmas tree hung with ornaments made by the Sunday school students from all the parishes—the Cathedral was beautiful.

At the altar burned the lantern lit in Armenia with the flame of St. Gregory. A table in the chancel held the parish lanterns that were going to be passed out that morning. It was moving to see all the lanterns lined up waiting to be lit. Then Father Mardiros arrived and he began to explain to me what was happening with the lanterns, how they were packaged, and what we were going to be doing with them. I asked if there was something I could do to help, and he told me that I had been chosen to give out communion.

When I heard that, I was "filled in my heart." I had never done the *Badarak* in the Cathedral, and now, this morning, I was going to be delivering Christmas communion. It was a thrill I had not expected.

Upon hearing that news, I walked towards the altar, and that's when I actually saw the flame flickering from the lantern. I had thought about the light of St. Gregory the Illuminator during all the crazy plotting and planning stages that had brought me to the Cathedral, but I had not actually thought about how I would feel when I saw it. In the moment I was awe-inspired. Even though the flame was only an inch or two tall, it seemed like it illuminated the whole sanctuary, including my presence, with the presence of Christ. The flame of the Illuminator seemed to be bringing Christ's words alive: "I am the light of the world. He who follows me will not walk in darkness, but will have the light of life."

I felt as if St. Gregory was there in spirit lifting that light out of the darkness of the pit and lifting it up for Armenia and Etchmiadzin and St. Vartan and for me and for everyone else to experience it and to receive it. This all happened in a split second, but from that moment on I enjoyed being there all the more, and I felt inspired by the presence of Christ.

People began to arrive—youth representatives, other priests, and parishioners. I sat down next to my teacher, Baron Krikor Vosganian, and I asked him if he wanted to sing something. He stood up and began singing a *sharagan* (hymn). I stood next to him and sang too. To be with him, to do with him what I had learned from him and to be doing it in the Cathedral in front of all those people from all the different parishes—it was wonderful.

The Bishop arrived, and the *Badarak* started, and there were a number of touching moments in the service, but as I got up to prepare communion during *Der Voghormia* (Lord, have mercy), I was especially struck by the young people seated in the front pews on the right side of the sanctuary. They were on their knees, and I could sense their joy, their anticipation, and their excitement over seeing this light and how profoundly it was affecting them.

Then we started offering communion. As I said, giving communion, in the Cathedral, on Christmas, the day of receiving the light—it was a privilege and a thrill.

Then the Bishop delivered his sermon. If this had been a black Baptist church, the people would have been on their feet clapping their hands and yelling praises. He was outstanding. He brought me to tears a couple of times, but when he told us how they had processed the light to Etchmiadzin with the President and other people in attendance and then to Yerevan Square where Lenin's statue once stood and now there stood a *khatchkar* (cross) and a lantern burning with the light of St. Gregory, I cried.

The youths received their lanterns during the service, but after the service the lanterns were to be blown out, because everyone was invited to attend a reception.

I didn't come to New York to have my lantern blown out.

My two youth representatives had received the flame from the Bishop, and that was the flame I wanted to take home.

I didn't attend the reception. Instead, I lit a votive candle from the youth lantern and I put the votive in a travel lantern and got ready to leave. On my way out the door of the Cathedral, I noticed that the votive was almost done, so I helped myself to nine more votives and a second travel lantern. I stabilized the travel lantern on the front passenger seat of my car and headed for Cleveland. Forty-five minutes later, I pulled over to the side of the road. I lit a new votive in the second travel lantern, cleaned out the old travel lantern, restocked it with a new votive, and hit the road again.

I did not know how long any of the votives would last. How long they burned seemed to depend on the air currents and movement of the car and how the wax burned. A votive could last anywhere from thirty minutes to two hours.

When I was driving, there came a point when it felt like it might have felt if I was in Bethlehem in the manger and Mary and Joseph had just said, "We are going to leave the stable for awhile. Will you watch the baby for us?" It felt like that. Thankfully, the next votive I put in lasted two hours, and I finally began to feel pretty good about my progress. Then it was as if St. Gregory was sitting in the car, saying, "The baby's safe. You can drive."

I lit the ninth votive 64 miles outside Cleveland, and, when I did, I knew I would make it. Back in Cleveland, I shared this story with the people of my parish because bringing the burning flame of St. Gregory to Cleveland was a mission for me. It was as if I were bringing Jesus and the gospel to the people through the light that had originally illuminated the hearts of the Armenian people. I had never experienced the light in my ministry in that way before.

†Reverend Father Haroutiun Dagley, *South Euclid, Ohio*

An Armenian Picnic in Seattle

I was born in Istanbul, Turkey, and I emigrated to the United States when I was a teenager. In 1960, I was drafted into the United States Army. I was stationed at Fort Lewis in Tacoma, Washington. In those days there were no Armenians in Tacoma, and I felt quite alone.

One day, when I had permission to leave the base, I went to Seattle. Whenever I was in a strange city I did two things. First, I would look for oriental rug dealers, because at that time the business was pretty much controlled by Armenians, and second, I would flip through the phone book searching for Armenian names. That day, I found an oriental rug shop listed in the phone book that had an American-sounding name, but I thought I'd stop by anyway. When I walked into the shop, I discovered that the owner was Armenian, but he hardly knew anything about Armenians. His family had been in this country for many years, and he didn't speak Armenian.

He did tell me that once a year the Armenians in the area got together for an Armenian picnic and that the picnic was coming up. A few weeks later, I went to the picnic. At the picnic, a doctor asked me if I spoke Armenian. I said I did. Then he asked me if I knew any Armenian church songs. I said I did. "Please sing something—anything," he said.

I sang, and, as I sang, tears filled the people's eyes. They knew nothing about Armenians. They did not speak one word of the Armenian language. They had no idea even if I was singing the *sharagan* correctly. But there were tears in their eyes. It was such a great feeling. I will never forget that day.

Sarkis Gennetian, *Watertown, Massachusetts*

Wanderings

I was born in Keorpe in Kharpert. I was eight years old when the Turks took my father away. Soon after he disappeared, the Turks announced the deportation of the women and children from our village. We were preparing for the death march when Turkish soldiers pulled me from my mother's side and took me to the house of a rich Turkish family where the daughter of the head of the family adopted me as her servant. I never saw my mother or my father again.

I was the youngest of three Armenian girls living and working in the wealthy Turkish family's home. The two other girls were named Markarid and Anna, and we spoke Armenian together while we did our chores. My life settled into a routine until it was time for the daughter I served to marry. She planned to move to a strange city where her husband's family lived and she wanted to take me with her. I panicked. I knew that if I went with her I would surely lose my language and my Armenian identity, because no Armenians were going to live in the new household except me. So I went to Markarid, the eldest of the three of us, and I asked her what I should do. By that time, the massacres were over and life in the village had settled down.

Markarid knew of two young Armenian brothers, Armenag and Kevork. They were in contact with Armenian organizations that were searching for boys and girls like me who had been taken from their parents by Turks and Kurds during the deportation. She asked me if I remembered the road I had traveled to get to the village where we were living. I said yes.

I can picture that road in my mind to this day.

"Take that road and walk straight until you approach the town of Bab [in Syria]. Before you enter the town, make a left turn. You will come to a factory. Ask for Armenag and Kevork. They will take care of you," Markarid said.

Alone, I left the house where I was living and walked down the road until I met a man. By that time I had learned to speak both Turkish and Arabic, so I asked him where the factory was. In Arabic, he told me to follow him. I did, but when I approached the factory I saw only Muslims wearing white turbans on their heads. Afraid, I ran home.

When Markarid saw me return, she reassured me that I was not in danger and she sent me back to the factory. Standing at the front gate of the factory for the second time that day, it took all the courage I had to ask for Armenag or Kevork. The man at the gate told me to wait. Soon a young man covered from head to toe with flour walked toward me. I think he thought that I had forgotten my language, because he addressed me in Turkish. Responding in Armenian, I told him that Markarid had sent me to him, so that he could send me to the Armenian orphanage in Aleppo.

Armenag took me to his house where he lived with his brother, Kevork, and their wives, who were sisters. I remember playing with Armenag's children. That was fun; after all, I was still only a child myself. But I did not stay with them long, because when the rich lady I had served found out I had run away, she put my name on a list of wanted people, so the Turkish authorities were looking for me and I was known to many people who lived in area. Finally, after I was chased a couple of times in the market by the Turks, Armenag arranged for me to go to the orphanage in Aleppo. Later, I moved from Aleppo to Cilicia, and finally I came to the United States, where my brother lived with his family.

I spent those many childhood years alone and wandering. As a child I did not understand much, but I believed in God and trusted He would protect me. Now, as an old lady, I know that I owe my entire life to His miracles. It was through His grace that I survived those years wandering from one household to another, from one village to another, and from one city to another until I finally came to America. It was through His miracle that I maintained my faith, my language, and my national identity. I think I was able to endure all the hardship because of my faith. The Turks were able to separate me from my parents, but, no matter what happened, I refused to be separated from my Armenian Apostolic Church.

Oghda Boghosian, *Fowler, California*

The Church in Yettem

Did you know that Yettem, California, is the only Armenian-named town in the United States? Yettem means "garden of paradise" in Armenian. Many Armenians, like my father's brother, settled in Yettem because the mountain-framed foothills of this part of California reminded them of home. My uncle came to this country before the massacres. He worked as a carpenter and helped build the original St. Mary's Armenian Church in Yettem in 1911.

My father survived the massacres. He joined his brother here after the war and began working as a carpenter, too. One night in 1947, tragedy hit our community. St. Mary's burned to the ground. We were devastated by the loss of our church, but we were also determined to rebuild it. My mother taught Sunday School in our home every Sunday morning until our new church was built, and my father helped build the church we have now. As a youngster, I remember him building the church altar in our garage. Today, everywhere I look in our church I see my father's handwork. It's one of the things that keeps me going.

Geraldine Simonian Hagopian, *Visalia, California*

My Father Loved Cowboy Movies

My father came to the United States before 1915 with a bunch of the boys from his hometown of Chunkush. He planned to go back. But, of course, after the massacres, there was nothing to go back to. His whole town was wiped out.

Like many who lost everything in the massacres, my father didn't like to talk about his home in Turkey much, but he did love watching cowboy movies. I asked him once, "Pa, how come you love cowboy movies so much?"

"It's not the cowboys I love," he said. "It's the scenery. The hills remind me of home."

Rose Zinakorjian, *Chicago, Illinois*

THE KID WHO DID NOT BECOME A PRIEST IN JERUSALEM

In 1890, a young man named Mihran Melikian from Izmir [Turkey] went to Jerusalem to study at the seminary to become a priest. At the seminary, he met another seminarian named Dikran Kasparian, and the two men became buddies. Before Melikian's graduation from the seminary, a family from Izmir arrived in Jerusalem on a pilgrimage, and he was assigned to take them around to the holy places. The family had a daughter, and young Melikian fell in love with her. The family returned to Izmir, but he could not get her out of his mind. Melikian graduated from the seminary, but he did not become a priest. He returned home to marry the girl who had stolen his heart.

Young Melikian was educated but poor, and the girl's family was rich. He knew that if he wanted to marry her, he needed to get a job and to succeed at it. In Izmir, he found a job working for a French shipping line operating out of the port; by 1906, he was the supervisor of the operation. As reward for pulling himself up by the bootstraps, Melikian married his beloved, with his buddy from seminary who did become a priest, Father Vartan Kasparian, performing the ceremony. Melikian was doing well. He and his new bride built the first house in Cordellio, an exclusive area located across the bay from Izmir, that was serviced with gas and electricity.

In the meantime, unsettling things were going on in the Armenian communities in the interior of the Ottoman Empire. Father Vartan decided to get out of the country, and he accepted an opening the church had for a priest in Fresno, California. Early in 1912, he left for California, vowing to report back to Melikian and to his brother, who lived with his family in Bursa, about life in America. Shortly after arriving in California, Father Vartan sent a wire telling them to gather up their families, leave everything behind, and join him in the United States.

The Melikian family and the Kasparian family of Bursa sold their homes and moved to Fresno where Father Vartan was the parish priest. They invested whatever money they came with into farms, and, like most people with no farming background, they lost it. After failing as a farmer, Melikian opened a grocery store.

Then, in 1917, Catholicos Papken Guleserian came to the United States. When he arrived in Fresno, he met his two former students from the seminary in Jerusalem—Father Vartan, the priest, and Melikian, the grocer. On his way to Fresno, the Catholicos had come through Los Angeles. He had visited with the small but rapidly growing Armenian community there which needed both a priest and church. "Hey Melikian, Kid Who Did Not Become a Priest in Jerusalem," he said. "You owe the nation and the church for your education. I'm going to ordain you into the priesthood and send you to Los Angeles."

Melikian replied, "Talk to my wife."

Catholicos Papken was able to convince them that they were needed more in Los Angeles in service to the church than as grocers in Fresno. He ordained Melikian into the priesthood, and, in 1918, Father Adom Melikian became the first Armenian priest in Los Angeles. He started a little church in a rented second-story auditorium located on the corner of 1st and Broadway. Over the next few years, the parish grew, and a guy named Antranig Caprielian became Treasurer of the Parish Council. He, Father Adom, and a carpenter by the name of Krikor Altunian decided to build a church.

To augment local fund-raising efforts, Father Adom made three trips across the country, picking up contributions that ranged from twenty cents to a few dollars from the more established Armenians in the East to help build the church in Los Angeles. In 1922, with his efforts to collect money, Caprielian's care of the finances, and Altunian's carpentry work, these three men built Holy Cross Armenian Church of Los Angeles for a total cost of $35,000. Today the Diocese and the Prelacy serve thousands of people throughout Southern California.

I can tell this story because Melikian, that young seminarian who did not become a priest in Jerusalem, and who years later was one of the founding fathers of the Armenian Apostolic Church in Los Angeles, was my maternal grandfather. One of the other founding father's, Antranig Caprielian, became my father-in-law when I fell in love with and married his daughter, Helen. Helen and I have been members of the church our whole lives and have been happily married for more than sixty years.

Oshyn Kasparian, *Los Angeles, California*

A Special Baptism

Archbishop Turian baptized me when I was three years old. He was a friend of my father's from the old country. After the massacres, he asked my father not to baptize any children he had until he came to America, because he wanted the honor of performing that sacrament for our family. That's why I wasn't baptized until 1932, when the Bishop came to the United States. The following Christmas Eve, he was killed at the altar in New York City during the celebration of *Badarak*. Archbishop Turian's murder is a dark page in the history of our church. Our church is still divided today because of it.

When I started attending the Fowler Church, Father Kevork asked me to tell him a little about myself so I told him this story. He looked at me like I was kidding him. Then I showed him my baptismal paper. Now I think he believes me.

Marilyn L. Pattigan, *Parlier, California*

Church Unity

We have a problem in our church. It's a divided church; we have a Prelacy and we have a Diocese. I grew up in a family affiliated with the Prelacy. In fact, I served for many years as chairman of the Prelacy Council, which is the top position for lay service in the Prelacy church structure. I became close to Archbishop Karekin Sarkissian when he was the Prelate in New York. He moved on to serve the church as the Catholicos of Cilicia in Lebanon and then as Catholicos of All Armenians in Etchmiadzin. So I had this experience not only with the Prelacy, but also with a man who was able to transcend the church's schism by occupying the highest position on both sides of the division. This perspective, combined with the independence of Armenia and the new conditions we live under here in America, convinced me that there is no longer any sense in perpetuating the church division.

I tried very hard when I was at the Prelacy to unite the church. As a representative from the Prelacy, I chaired the Unity Committee from the beginning of that joint church effort for almost twenty years. Political circumstances, primarily, prevented that effort from succeeding.

During that time, and especially after Armenia's independence in 1991, the homeland opened to the Diaspora. Like many other people, I visited Armenia numerous times for a variety of reasons. As I did, I began to recognize that my true allegiance was to Armenia. Then, when Karekin Catholicos of Cilicia was elected Catholicos of All Armenians and took up residency in Etchmiadzin, my slow yet natural progression away from the Prelacy towards the Diocese continued. When the Diocese asked me to chair the 1700th Anniversary Celebration Planning Committee, I accepted the position as a logical continuation of my lifelong service to the church.

I just quietly moved over.

I have told my close friends how normal a transition this should be. People should not think of it as a great leap. I have heard comments, of course. A few people have called me all kinds of names. Some have said that I'm a turncoat. That's old-style thinking. That's not the type of thinking that should prevail today. I overlook these comments and just keep doing what I am doing—on my own.

Back to the unity issue: The Armenian people were all for unity, but they were looking to the leadership to make the move. It was the leadership that failed. The leadership did not have the courage to make the decision and bring about the formal unification of the church. Although the membership wanted unity, the people felt powerless to force the issue upon their leaders. Given this, I now believe that the Armenian community as we know it today needs to focus on strong leadership. It's not always bottom-up. It's also top-down.

Karekin Catholicos I was an inspiration to me. He taught me, among other things, to lead by example. I hope in my small way I am setting an example for others to make the church one again.

Michael Haratunian, *Glen Head, New York*

Working for Armenia

My daily ritual is working for Armenia. It has always been a part of my life and my husband's life, but since independence it's been a daily labor of love.

In 1984, when I first went to Armenia, we arrived in daylight. On the drive from the airport to Etchmiazdin, I saw my father and my mother reflected everywhere in the yards and habits of the people along the route. I grew up in Connecticut. We had a huge yard. My father grew many different kinds of fruits and vegetables, and he had a huge grape arbor. He took such pride in trimming those grapes. As we drove past, I saw people trimming their grape arbors like my father did. I saw them sweeping their yards with hand-made brooms made out of tree branches tied together—the same brooms my father made and used in our yard in Connecticut. That day, on that ride to Etchmiadzin, I recognized my parents everywhere and I wept.

Working for Armenia is something I feel I have to do. It makes me feel good, and I know that my parents are happy about this too, even though they've been deceased for a long time now.

Julie Ashekian, *Kensington, Connecticut*

Birth of a Parish

MetroWest, the newly established parish in the Eastern Diocese of the Armenian Church of America in the area of Eastern Massachusetts known as MetroWest, was born out of an innocent conversation a few of us had one evening. While sitting around the table, it occurred to us that we were friends because of the experiences we shared through the life of the church as children and as young adults. It wasn't a stretch for us to look at our own children and ask how they were going to get a similar experience.

One of the main problems we faced was that we all lived in an area of Massachusetts around Framingham called MetroWest. The nearest Armenian Church was a forty-minute drive to either Worcester or Watertown, and for most of us the trek to church every Sunday was not happening on a regular basis.

I was a deacon at the time. That night we decided to get together once a month at people's homes, do a *Jashou* (Meal) Service, enjoy some fellowship, and get our kids together. Twenty of us met the following month, but we soon grew into a group of thirty. With the increasing attendance at our *Jashou* Services, we realized that a parish in the area might be something people wanted. We petitioned the Bishop to become a Mission Parish, and in September 1998 we held our first service as a Mission Parish. That's how MetroWest began.

Early on, we recognized that we faced the opportunity to build a faith community from the ground up, and we felt that it was important to accept that challenge head on.

We recognized that we were dealing with many mixed marriages—Armenians married to non-Armenians. We were cognizant of the fact that most second- and third- and fourth-generation Armenians do not speak Armenian. We wanted to design an Armenian Apostolic faith experience that speaks to the American Armenian or Armenian American, whichever you prefer. In order to do that, we needed to be willing to change a few things.

I was clear from the start that, if people were looking to change the Armenian Church, I was not interested. From the beginning, the mandate of MetroWest was to make the Armenian Church significant in the life of every member. Our mandate was not to change anything in the Church, but to present our Church in a way that people could relate to. So, at MetroWest, we made three important changes.

First, we changed the language of the *Badarak* into English. Not only that, but we changed the English into understandable English. We took all of the words that nobody understands in English, like "anathematize" and "covetousness," and replaced them with words that people could follow. "Anathematize" means "to condemn," so I use the word "condemn." I translated "covetousness" as "resentful desire."

The second thing we did was shorten the length of the service. At MetroWest, we start the *Badarak* at 9:30 a.m., and the Liturgy ends no later than 11:00 a.m. Let's face it, in many of the parishes across the country, when the *Badarak* starts at 10:00 and ends at 12:30, most people don't arrive at church until 11:30. So we said, "Let's try to get a faith experience where people will come for the entire *Badarak*." The shortened Liturgy works. The only thing I leave out is the preparation of the priest and the gifts, and I don't actually leave it out; I do it before people arrive.

The third and possibly the most important change we made at MetroWest was instituting the concept of family worship. Children attend the *Badarak* with their families, and they stay in church until after communion. Prior to confession, I call the children up to the front of the church. We sit down together, and I talk to them as their Der Hayr, giving them a brief lesson. The kids and I have a unique rapport going, and I think that's because I spend time with them every Sunday during the *Badarak*.

After the lesson, the children and their Sunday School teachers receive communion first. Then they go to Sunday School while the rest of the congregation takes communion. I make my announcements, deliver the sermon, and, if there's *hokehankist* (requiem), we do *hokehankist*. The service ends and we go to fellowship where the children meet us after Sunday School.

With these changes, we found that the people at MetroWest worship as an entire community. Ninety-nine percent of the people take communion every Sunday. Our worship is a living experience in which everybody participates.

Participation in the Liturgy is very important to us. Another thing we have done to encourage participation is not have a formal choir. Instead, about five or six people lead the congregation in song. All of the hymns are maintained in Armenian. With the *Badarak* in English and the hymns in Armenian, it's a great mix of the two languages, and it allows the congregation to understand what's going on and to participate. The *Badarak* is really a moving experience when you witness total participation from the congregation.

Finally, we do a lot of outreach. We work through the Department of Social Services in the Framingham area to help people in need at all the major holidays, and about six times a year we volunteer at the Salvation Army soup kitchens in our area. We believe in service and outreach, not only to the Armenian community, but also to the local community.

In less than three years as a Mission Parish, our membership has grown to more than one hundred. We have more than sixty children enrolled in Sunday School. I have fifteen kids in my youth group. Given our success, we petitioned the Diocese, and we are now a full parish.

As one might expect, MetroWest has its critics. Many people say that when you change the language of the Liturgy you lose the Armenian. Many contend that we might as well go to the Catholic or Protestant Church. This opinion assumes our entire liturgical experience is tied to the language and that what makes us Armenian Apostolic Christians is only the language. Both of these assertions are wrong.

At MetroWest, we try to meet the needs of our people. It's not that we want to abandon our Armenianism or our Armenian heritage. Rather, we hope to present our Church in all its beauty and wonder in a way that Armenians living in America can relate to. MetroWest is about how we express our faith, not about changing the faith. The reason we made the changes we did is because we are loyal to our Armenian Christian heritage. If we weren't loyal, the people would just go to other churches. If we weren't loyal, the families of the mixed marriages would go to the spouse's church. So it's about being loyal to the Armenian Church, but it's also about creating an Armenian American religious experience.

One of the unfortunate characteristics of Armenian people is that we are willing to add to what we do, but we don't like to take anything away. We are afraid of change. Without change we become stale and stagnant. I believe that our faith here in America has become stagnant. We talk about the living faith, but, if you go into our churches, more often than not we speak about the past. If the people in our history spoke only about the past, we would not have Gomidas, Ekmalian, or Nersess Shnorhali today. We have these people's contributions because, rather than dwelling on the past, they became the living faith of their time, and they contributed to our religious experience and heritage.

Gomidas wrote his *Badarak* in the 1920s in Turkey. That's modern history, but, if you consider our life experience since Gomidas wrote his *Badarak* and as Armenians living in the United States, everything about our lives has changed since then. Where are the new prayers? Where is the new growth? People have said to us at MetroWest, "You cannot change the *Badarak*. How can we change perfection?" I say, "Love, if it's misdirected, can be a suffocating force."

So, if we're talking about a living faith, we have to speak to our daily lives, and our daily lives six days a week are very foreign to the two-hour service we attend on Sunday morning. That Sunday morning for many people is a trip back into history, and I don't think that is what the *Badarak* is supposed to be all about. Those of us seated around that dinner table didn't think so. Given the realities of our life and our commitment to the Armenian Church, we accepted the challenges of building a faith community where we lived, and we made the changes we felt would help us experience our faith in a more immediate way and which would offer our children the chance to have the experiences and relationships we had growing up.

The bottom line is that most of us at MetroWest feel our Christianity is more important than our Armenianism. Armenianism is the way in which we express our Christianity. St. Gregory was not an Armenian. He suffered and evangelized the Armenians because of his Christianity. As Armenians living here in America, we need to emphasize that we are expressing our Christianity through our culture.

I know a lot of clergymen who wanted to do this but didn't have the opportunity to do it. When the opportunity came to me, I thought, "Somebody's got to do this," because I really believe, if we don't do something that speaks to some of the issues and concerns we've tried to address at MetroWest, in about twenty years many of our churches in this country will be museums. There is a ton of opposition to this whole situation, but I invite people come to MetroWest. Come and experience it, because it is a different experience.

Reverend Father Krikor Sabounjian, *Holliston, Massachusetts*

Sacrifice

My mother was a very pious woman. She was always reading the Bible and books of prayers. She often told me how my father would go to the church to light candles after he finished his work in the fields. We were such a pious family in those days, but modern times are different. These modern times have brought our people spiritual famine.

For example, in Lebanon during the Pentecost, people rose at 3 o'clock in the morning to gather together and pray. As a child, I attended these prayer meetings. Often the faithful got so excited at these meetings that they fainted. Those incidents deeply impressed and influenced me. During Lent, many people, especially women, faithfully abstained from eating all day until after sunset. They, too, influenced me.

Shortly after I moved to the United States, I said to Father Dajad, "What is this? People are not abstaining on Wednesdays or Fridays or on other occasions." He told me that fasting was difficult in the United States. I found his words strange and it upset me to hear them. But he was right. No matter what you do or where you go, whether it's a wedding or a funeral or a meeting, eating is an inseparable part of the event. It's all about food.

I continue to observe the forty-day Lenten fast, and I think we owe our souls this much of a sacrifice. My mother used to say, "The mouth should not consume everything; some should be left to the face." She meant that we have to attend to our spiritual needs as well as our physical needs. I had parents who taught me the importance of sacrifice. I fear that we may have come to a point where we have forgotten what we have learned.

Siran Kassabian, *Watertown, Massachusetts*

The Story of a Mission Parish

I am Armenian, but I am not, nor have I ever been, a member of the Armenian Apostolic Church. I was born an Episcopalian, and I occupy a comfortable pew in the Episcopal Church. Over a quarter of a century ago, Archbishop Manoogian planted the seed for an Armenian Apostolic Mission Parish in Albuquerque, New Mexico. My motivation to be involved in the effort was to help provide an opportunity for Armenians who are not churched to come in contact with the church. I believe that the church is the nucleus of the Armenian nation everywhere in the world, and, if I can play some little role in that happening, then that is what I want to do.

My involvement in the parish mission program began on Archbishop Manoogian's first trip to New Mexico. I was assigned to pick him up in Santa Fe. On our way back from the airport, there was a car wreck on the highway. We were not involved in the accident, but the Archbishop asked me to stop. I pulled over, and he got out of the car to speak to the people involved in the wreck. Like magic, the situation calmed down. I was so impressed with him that, when he got back in the car, I told him that he reminded me of my father. I lost my father as a young boy, and, until that day, I have never said that to any one else in my life. The Archbishop impressed me as a man of real faith, and loyalty to him may be another reason I have stayed involved in the Mission Parish here.

We used my parish, St. Mark's Episcopal Church, to host Archbishop Manoogian's *Badarak* that day, and we have used it to host four services a year since then. Roughly one hundred families are on our Mission Parish mailing list, and about thirty folks attended the Lighting of the Candles 1700th Anniversary service.

Developing the Mission Parish in Albuquerque has been a slow, continuous effort. After twenty-six years of being involved, I have to admit that I still really don't understand the Liturgy. Bridging the language problem and teaching the significance of the Liturgy needs to be a continuous focus.

Over the decades, I've attended numerous sessions with visiting clergy to consider ideas about how to appeal to more people. Forgive me for saying this, but, although I've suggested Bible Study classes and other things that I know work in the Episcopal community, in my experience those things don't seem to be as important as raising money. Money has always stuck out to me as a high objective for the church. It's been my experience that, if people come and participate, the money will follow.

We've also had some difficulty with getting someone assigned to us as the mission coordinator from the Diocese. In the last several years we've had five or six different guys. That tends to slow down the process.

On the positive side...several years ago, a retired Episcopal clergyman by the name of Norm Abrams and his wife started attending St. Mark's. One day, Norm confided to me that he had been born a Toufinkian and that he was really an Armenian in disguise. As an ordained retired Episcopal priest of Armenian heritage, he offered to give pastoral care to our local Armenian community when no one is available from New York. This is a very positive development for our community—so another piece of the mission church is now in place.

Archbishop Manoogian came to New Mexico in the 1970s trying to gather the Armenian flock. More than a quarter of a century later, our Mission Parish is still in the process of coming to fruition. I am optimistic for the future, and looking back I am able to see the Lord's hand in all that has taken place over these years.

Greg Devejian, *Albuquerque, New Mexico*

The Question of Survival

I definitely question the survival of the Armenian Church. Over the last two months, I've been working on a documentary for public television on the Armenians as survivors. During my research, I have found and personally talked with representatives of Armenian communities all over the world. We are everywhere—Thailand, Denmark, Bulgaria—and everywhere we are struggling to survive.

How is the church going to survive if the Armenians don't survive? The church hasn't survived in Ani or in Van or in Mush or in Kars. Do you know what has happened to our churches there? I can show you pictures. They are barns filled with hay and cows. The *khatchkars* (stone crosses) have been ripped out or burned black. People living in those villages today use them to construct the walls of their homes. You have a pile of stones, then a *khatchkar*, more stones, and another *khatchkar*. That's what has happened to our churches in Eastern Anatolia.

It used to be the church that helped our communities form and survive. My concern right now, however, is to survive as an Armenian. Today, if we survive as Armenians, the church will follow. Some people may believe that, if the church survives, Armenians will survive. At this point, I think the church is not a strong enough power within the community to help us survive the test of time. We need to continue with our language and our culture, and we need to support Armenia and the people who live there.

Let me tell you something—we have enemies. Analysts at the Brookings Institution, a world-renowned political think tank, have told me that a lot of people believe that the Armenians and Armenia will not survive. They point to the mass exodus of people from Armenia that began with independence and that is still going on today. The dramatic loss of population in the Republic of Armenia has not gone unnoticed by our enemies. The Azeris and the Turks know that the Armenians are going to leave Karabagh. They know that the Armenians are leaving Armenia. Why should we lose more men fighting for those lands? They think, Why not just sit back and wait for the Armenians to move to Los Angeles? Then we can move right in.

Okay, it's not going to happen in the next two years. But the person from the Brookings Institution thinks it may happen between the next ten to twenty years. Hey! Wait a minute! That's my generation!

Shant Petrossian, *New York, New York*

Understanding the Liturgy

My father is Dutch and English; my mother is Armenian. I was baptized in the Armenian Church and then brought up in Baptist and Congregational Protestant Sunday Schools. As a child, my exposure to being Armenian was at holiday gatherings with my mother's side of the family. The relatives would come over; they'd speak Armenian; we'd eat Armenian food. After the meal, the musicians in the family would break out the *dumbeg* and *oud* and begin to play Armenian folk songs in the living room while the rest of the family sang and danced.

Occasionally, we went to Sunday morning worship at the Armenian Church, but I didn't understand what was going on, and it didn't seem like worship to me, because in the Protestant Church everyone participates. There are congregational responses and readings. People open their hymnals and sing together. I've even seen people break out pens and paper and take notes during the sermon.

In the Armenian Church, it seemed like everybody was involved in his or her own special kind of meditation. I didn't understand the language; the music was heavy; the air was filled with smoke and smell of incenses: that wasn't what church was about to me. The *Badarak* didn't make a whole lot of sense, and, when I asked people what was going on—why you had to stand and sit, why the curtain opened and closed—nobody had any answers. Sorry to say, but I didn't get really good answers even from the priests I asked. Mostly, I got attitude—the Armenian Apostolic Church is the true church; my Baptist roots weren't viable—things like that. That doesn't encourage people to come.

So I always returned to the Protestant Church, but I kept my social ties with the Armenians—through student associations, going to Kef dances, and hitting the bazaars. Then, one day during a period when I was attending a variety of services on Sundays, helping out with the Armenian Church Youth Organization, and volunteering as a coach at the Andover High School, Father Yeprem Kelegian asked me what I was doing. As usual, Father Yeprem made me think, and, upon discerning reflection and prayer, I decided to go into the seminary. I enrolled at Andover-Newton Theological School, a Protestant seminary in Newton, Massachusetts.

In my second year at seminary, I was required to do a project for a class, and I chose to study the foundations of the *Badarak*. Through this study, I wrote a paper that compared baptism and communion in the Baptist tradition with the sacraments of baptism and communion in the Armenian tradition, and my heart and my mind opened. The beauty and the richness and the history of the Armenian Liturgy touched me, and I finally understood what was and is intended for the faithful in those pews on Sunday mornings.

I knew then that I wanted to serve in the Armenian Church and to help people get the Divine Liturgy. The people don't get it. I want to help people get it.

Now that I am a priest, once in a while during *Badarak*, I stop and explain what's going on in the Liturgy. I tell my parish about the significance of a hymn or a prayer. For example, we have a prayer about the Ascension, and, when it is said during the *Badarak*, at that moment in the service, we are revering Christ's holiness as He goes up and is one with his Holy Father. Once I explain what is happening, people can recognize that, when that prayer is being said, a holy moment is taking place because Christ is leaving the earthly and going to the Heavenly. I don't do this every week, but I do it as often as is helpful, because I want people to learn and get it.

I guess where I do the most instruction is in our youth programs. I like to do hands-on things with the kids. I bring them into the church and let them touch some things. I talk about a saint whose picture is on the wall or I tell them why we wash the feet of the faithful on Holy Thursday. I want the kids to feel like the church is their home. I want them to see me not as a person who wears a forbidding black shirt with a white collar but as a person who can be approached. Maybe it's my Protestant roots, but I believe that, if our worship service has meaning, and it's just as much a part of our children's lives as watching Barney on TV or going to preschool, we can build on that.

†**Reverend Father Haroutiun Dagley,** *South Euclid, Ohio*

Learning About the Faith from My Children

A generation gap may exist in our church. Those in the younger generation seem to be closer to the church spiritually and theologically than those of us born to the first generation of Armenian Americans, who seem more tied to the church because of heritage and nationalistic feelings.

I received my various ranks in the church over many years. My knowledge of the Liturgy and the sacraments is largely self-taught and came as a result of my participation, which began at age eight as a candleholder at St. James Armenian Church in Watertown, Massachusetts, and culminated in my ordination to the diaconate in 1969. Then my children, led by my oldest son, began to focus on the teachings of Christ and what it means to be a Christian. As they learned, they began to share the teachings of the church with me. I would say that, before my three children found their faith, I was a liturgical deacon in the church, and, as my children's faith blossomed, my insight into the orthodox doctrine opened also. I'm very thankful for what I've learned from them.

Deacon Allan Y. Jendian, *Fresno, California*

I Go to Church for Me

I go to church to worship God with other Armenian Christians. I participate in the mass. If I'm in the congregation, I sing in the congregation. If I'm in the choir that day, I sing with the choir. I kneel. I pray. I participate in the Holy Eucharist. I drink the wine, and I eat the bread.

It's easy in our church to just be an onlooker. The *Badarak* is not a quick service. It's up to each person to take an active part in the Liturgy.

†**Carla Donobedian,** *Fresno, California*

Problems with the Priest

When I was a young mother, I left my parish because of something that had happened concerning the priest. For a period of time after that, I traveled twenty miles on Sunday mornings with my two little children in the back seat of the car to another parish. Finally, my father asked me why I was going so far, especially with the children, because he was concerned that something might happen on the road. My father's question forced me to think about what I was doing and why. I realized that you don't go to the church for the priest. You go for yourself and your family. I came to my senses and returned closer to home.

I see people now leaving churches. They don't like the organist. They are not being paid attention to. I was there once. It's not right.

Virginia Kasparian, *Selma, California*

Prepared to Lead

The role of a leader is difficult. I found out just how difficult the summer I became a Land and Culture Organization site leader in Armenia. I had worked on a church renovation project as a group member for two summers before it was my turn to lead the group, so I thought I was prepared. I knew the project and what work still needed to be done. I had been a popular member in the previous groups, and I was able to quickly befriend the local villagers. I thought I was going to be the best leader Land and Culture had ever seen.

Then we got to Armenia. When I was one of the group members, no matter what we had done the night before or how tired we were, we got up every morning and started work at 9:00 a.m. Our group leader said to get up, so we did. But that summer, when I was the leader, the people in my group did not want to get out of bed and go to work.

I wasn't prepared for that. I was prepared if someone fell and injured their knee. I was prepared to not have enough food. I was prepared to make the volunteers' experience memorable, but I was not prepared for the possibility of group members not wanting to get up and do the work. So when it happened, I was completely lost.

It seems to me that the situation I faced in Armenia that summer is similar to what our priests are facing today. Going to church should just be part of us as Armenians, but many in our community, including myself, do not feel the need to go to church. My experience as a group leader for Land and Culture taught me how difficult it is to make someone do something that they should just want to do, but don't.

I can understand why our priests are not prepared to confront this problem—because it has rarely happened in the past. Our priests seem prepared to handle one person who feels that way, to bring them into the church and visit them in the home, but they are not prepared for the numbers that present themselves today. Our Der Hayrs have a very tough task ahead of them, and I'm hoping they are able to take on this challenge. I'm all for keeping traditions alive, but times are changing, and, in my opinion, the church may need to accept a compromise and make some changes to increase attendance, especially in my generation.

Shant Petrossian, *New York, New York*

Throw It Up to the Lord

In any given situation, after I think I've done everything I can possibly do, I throw it up to the Lord. I say, "You know what, Lord? Done all I can do. It's up to you."

Normally, what the Lord does is offer me opportunities. I believe in destiny, but I also believe we all have free will. We are given opportunities and the freedom to choose which way to go. An example of this process at work in my life is the journey my husband and I have been on that has led us to greater faith and to the desire to do more and more service for the Lord and our church.

When I was a child, my father was chairman of the Board of Trustees of our church, but the religious end of it was never explained to me or my sisters. For me, growing up in the church meant show up late, check out what people are wearing, leave early. Then, when I was first married, my husband was working very hard; he worked most Sundays, so we rarely went to church. Even after the kids were born, we were part of the Christmas/Easter crowd.

Then, one Sunday, I took the kids to Armenian School. During dropoff, a friend of mine pointed to a guy dressed in a running suit, and she told me that he was a priest. I looked at my friend and said, "No way is that guy an Armenian priest. He is speaking English. He has no accent and he's my age."

"Yeah, he is," she said.

"Okay. Introduce us."

I met Father Haroutiun Dagley, and he confirmed that he was the priest at a parish located about a forty-minute drive from where we live. I was so intrigued with this priest-who-didn't-look-or-act-like-a-priest that, a few Sundays later, I packed the kids into the car and drove the distance to attend his *Badarak*. When I got home, I told my husband that he had to meet him.

My husband took the next Sunday off, and we went as a family to church. My husband met Father Haroutiun, and he really liked him, because he reminded him of an Armenian-speaking Danish priest that he knew at the orphanage in Beirut where he had been raised.

For the next year, we went to church as a family. During that time, some issues arose in the parish, and a time came when there were no deacons serving with Father Haroutiun at the altar. After watching him opening curtains, closing curtains, and doing the whole service himself, my husband asked him if he would like some help. Father Haroutiun was thrilled.

The following Sunday, my husband put on a *shabig* (robe) and began to participate at the altar. Soon he was ordained a deacon.

When Father Haroutiun moved to a church in Cleveland, we began to attend a local parish. Our two children go with us to church every Sunday, and they are very much involved in understanding what it means to be an Armenian Apostolic Christian and to have the faith, something I learned after the age of forty. Through this process, slowly my husband began to realize that he was being called to more service of our Lord, and he decided to become a priest.

I am very proud of him. I couldn't imagine a person better suited to serve the Lord. He has the right temperament for the job. He has the faith and he has the desire. I think it's divine intervention plus my husband's response to the opportunities presented to him that brought his faith forward.

Of course, he's totally different from me. I'm a little loud, a little exuberant. I think the funniest thing that has happened on this amazing journey happened during my husband's ordination service into the diaconate. Standing in front of the congregation, the Archbishop said that one never knows where this could lead…that one day my husband could decide to become a Der Hayr. When he said that, instead of looking at my husband, everyone in the church turned around and looked at me, because it wasn't as odd to think of my husband as a priest as it was to think of me as a *yeretzgin*.

Sandy Soulakian, *Chicago, Illinois*

Who Is Armenian?

When I was at graduate student at the University of Southern California, I belonged to the Armenian Students Association (ASA). At one meeting, the topic of Armenian identity came up. In general, the foreign-born students in the group seemed to believe that, if a person did not speak Armenian, that person was less Armenian than someone who did speak the language. As a less-than-fluent Armenian speaker, I found this a very difficult discussion to participate in. However, once I had time to process the attitudes and opinions that had been expressed during the meeting, I decided to formally research the topic of Armenian identity as part of my doctoral thesis in sociology.

For my dissertation, I identified six aspects of Armenian identity—speaking Armenian, knowing Armenian history, being active in Armenian organizations, feeling proud of one's Armenian heritage, identifying with Armenian people, and having Armenian parents—and I asked a wide sampling of Armenians living in the United States, ranging in age from young to old, to rank these aspects of Armenian identity according to priority.

My research revealed that people hold different concepts of who or what makes a person Armenian depending on the generation they belong to. Like the foreign-born students in my ASA chapter, the foreign-born Armenians who participated in my study tended to rank speaking Armenian toward the top of the list. This same trait tended to fall toward the bottom of the priority list for many American-born Armenians. Second-generation Armenians ranked having Armenian parents a much higher priority than did Armenians born in later generations. Later generations ranked feeling proud and identifying with Armenians highest among the six choices.

I discovered that Armenian identity changes with each generation.

I think that this is an important discovery and that the community needs to acknowledge and honor the differences in perception held by the different members of the community of what makes a person Armenian, because, unfortunately, we can be a very judgmental people. For example, how accepting are we of people who do or do not speak Armenian? How accepting are we of non-Armenian spouses? How accepting are we of the children of those intermarriages?

Let me share an unfortunate example of how this judgment played out at an Armenian Church Youth Organization (ACYO) basketball game. I was trying to get a distant relative of mine involved in ACYO activities. His mother is Armenian and his father is German. He does not speak Armenian and he does not look Armenian. In fact, at the time, he was a sixteen-year-old kid with a cap of blond hair who stood over six feet tall, loved to play basketball, and was good at it. As he played, people on the opposite team's bench began to question his Armenian descent. Who is that kid? He's not Armenian.

What an impact that one incident had on that young man's life. He was so hurt that his roots had been denied and that he was the subject of a controversy, that he never participated in another ACYO activity. He is not a member of the church or the community today.

I don't know what it is, but we tend to be an exclusive group, and that is not the Christian way. It's stories like the one I just told about my relative's experience in the community that led many to believe that the Armenian community as well as the Armenian church are losing more members than they are gaining when intermarriage occurs. That is unfortunate. We have so much to gain by broadening the circle rather than limiting it. If we continue making it exclusive, we are going to exclude ourselves to death. Intermarriage is inevitable. My doctoral thesis proves that Armenian identity changes with each generation. It's time we broaden our definition of who counts as Armenian.

Matthew Ari Jendian, Ph.D., *Clovis, California*

Respecting the Diversity Among Us

As a Yeretzgin, I have had the opportunity to get to know Armenians from all over the world. In my experience, there is great cultural diversity among people of Armenian heritage. I've noticed that many of the differences seem to depend on where a person was born and raised. The culture and customs of the birth country seem to affect how different groups of us feel, act, and behave. I was born in Soviet Georgia, and I now live in the United States, so I feel most comfortable sharing examples of how Armenians from Armenia tend to have different expectations and act differently from American-born Armenians when confronted with similar situations.

In general, when Armenians from Armenia face difficulties, they expect others to try to help and comfort them. That does not seem to be true for the majority of Armenians born in the United States. For example, when an Armenian from Armenia is sick, he or she expects others to visit. I would go as far as to say that, if people do not come and visit the person who is ill, the ill person is likely to be offended. I remember when my cousin was sick. She took pride in the fact that many people came and visited her. "Now I know who will come when I die," she said. Visitors were an indication that the community cared for her.

In addition to expecting and receiving visitors, the person who is sick or members of the family are expected to offer their guests some hospitality. Coffee is prepared and something sweet to eat is put out on the table. This hospitality and the socializing that goes with it lightens the mood, helps divert everyone's attention from the illness, and provides support for the family.

I had to learn that Armenians born in the United States tend not to want to talk about or share their experiences with illness. I sense that they feel that sharing their health problems somehow burdens others. This, at least in their minds, is unacceptable. In general, I've found that Armenians born in America do not want to be visited when they are sick. Instead, they prefer a phone call, get well cards, flowers, or even some candy as opposed to being seen in person.

This difference between these two groups of Armenians also seems to apply to the area of money. Often Armenians from Armenia ask to borrow money from their close relatives. But no matter how small a loan is needed, American-born Armenians will go to a bank for a loan rather than ask someone they know for financial assistance. Perhaps this difference stems from the two countries' banking systems. Today in Armenia, a few banks do offer loans, but historically bank loans did not exist, so people from Armenia are used to giving or receiving loans from each other, while in the United States bank loans are commonplace and accessible.

I have also noticed that Armenians born in Armenia and Armenians born in the United States differ in how they relate to God. Armenians from Armenia call upon God's help for every little event that happens in life. They write special prayers. They offer special vows of thankfulness when prayers have been answered. They thank God frequently and in many small ways. That does not seem to be the way that American-born Armenians relate to God. Rather than thanking God often in small ways, they seem to prefer to give larger gifts less frequently. The two groups thank God equally but in very different ways.

In short, it seems to me that those born in Armenia tend to reach out to others during difficult times. They ask for comfort and help, while those born in the United States try to be more self-sufficient. In my work, I've discovered that we have a lot in common, but we are very different, too, and it is important to respect the different feelings and cultures represented within our community.

Yeretzgin Mariam Dingilian, *Irvine, California*

Reverse Assimilation

When people ask my children what nationality they are, they say, "Armenian." I laugh. It doesn't bother me. Often, I forget I'm not.

Lauren Chalekian, *Racine, Wisconsin*

Cultural Background Makes a Difference

I'm from Egypt. Even though Egypt had thirty thousand Armenians at the time, there was no such thing as an "Armenian section" in Alexandria or Cairo. We lived in mixed-nationality neighborhoods among Arabs, Greeks, Italians, French, and others. But the Armenians from Lebanon generally lived in concentrated Armenian communities, so their identity as "Armenians" was different from mine.

Then there are the Armenians from Turkey. Again, they are different. We Armenians from the Middle East tend to emphasize the Genocide, whereas the Armenians from Bolis were not as exposed to what happened in 1915. Consequently, the Genocide is a crucial part of the spirituality of Middle Eastern Armenians, whereas it plays a different role for many from Bolis. In addition, Middle Eastern–born Armenians come from cultures that are less homogenous than Armenians born in the United States or Armenia. As a result, how they relate to each other and how they express their spirituality is different.

When I was a parish pastor, I was very aware of the cultural differences among my parishioners, and I discovered that I had to address the same topic differently with the different groups. For example, for Armenians born in the United States, I used to give an evening lecture on the topic of aging parents with adult children. They loved to attend that kind of talk, and the chairs in the lecture hall were filled. In contrast, the subject is a non-issue for Armenians from Armenia, because, in the vast majority of the cases, the adult children just accept that they will care for their aging parents. Finally, many of the Armenians from the Middle East are not really sure how to handle the issue. Unfortunately, they won't come to a seminar, so, to address the subject, I found that I had to go to each home and discuss the situation and the options with each family.

We Armenians are a diverse group, and, in my work as a priest and as a researcher, I've found that it is important to understand the root of our differences in order to celebrate them and to make them venues for stronger spirituality and greater unity.

Reverend Father Stepanos Dingilian, Ph.D., *Irvine, California*

Stuffed Vegetables

Despite living in Milwaukee, Wisconsin, we ate Armenian food most nights for dinner. My mother prepared okra all different ways, and she routinely served stuffed vegetables.

Why ruin a vegetable by stuffing it with something? Stuffed vegetables are not American, and a part of me hated it. Every once in a while, my dad would pick up the big serving spoon and clank it on the side of the pot. "See this?" he'd say. "This is real food. What do you think the Americans are eating tonight?" Visions of hamburgers and French fries would dance into my mind. "Ha!" my father would snort. "You call that food?"

I spent much of my youth trying to figure out how to have a meal in which the meat was separated from the vegetables on the plate. Everything about my upbringing, from religion to food, made me Armenian. In my home it was the American culture that was foreign.

Reverend Father Yeprem Kelegian, *Racine, Wisconsin*

Sunday Drives

My father was one of the few Armenian men who drove an automobile during the Depression years. Every Sunday afternoon after church, he would gather my sisters and my mother into the car, and we would go for a ride. When we were out of the city and on the highway, he'd say, "Okay girls, let's sing." And we'd sing *Der Voghormia* (Lord, have mercy) and other church songs as we drove through the countryside outside of Racine.

Mary Stevoff, *Chicago, Illinois*

Rank and File

During the core of the *Badarak*, when consecrating the bread and wine, our priest takes off his crown and mantle. During the consecration, our bishop takes off his crown, too, and becomes a regular priest. Why do our clergy remove their symbols of rank during our service? Because, in truth, we are all servants of the church, we each serve different functions, and none of us is meaningful without the others. The women in the kitchen, the guy on the council who counts the money, and the people who sing in the choir—together we make the church.

Dr. Dennis R. Papazian, *Troy, Michigan*

Silent Service and Support

Let's face it, serving on church and community committees takes time away from your family. I have been able to serve for as long and as consistently as I have because of my wife's love and understanding. She may not have been on any of the committees, but she was always there, behind the scenes, supporting me.

Early in our marriage, she taught school while I went back to college to get my degree. When we started a family, she was content to be home with the children. She managed the home and arranged our family schedule so that we were able to participate fully in all the activities we wanted to participate in. Over the years, we have entertained many people in our home as part of our service to the community. She's a great hostess and makes everyone feel welcome. I owe a lot to my wife.

Deacon Allan Y. Jendian, *Fresno, California*

My Little Angel

I am the volunteer, administrative director for the Children of Armenia Sponsorship Program. The program is a Women's Guild Central Council project of the Eastern Diocese. Our sponsors support 1800 children living in Armenia, and we take care of an orphanage that has more than 140 children in residence. In the decade or so that I've been involved in the program, I feel blessed to have been able to watch so many children grow up. They are all precious, but, from the first day, I made eye contact with one particular little boy in the orphanage.

Most children at the orphanage have no parents, but some children are there on a temporary basis. That was the case with this little boy and his sister. When the children lost their father, their mother left them at the orphanage with the understanding that when she got on her feet she would take them back. She had since remarried, but, in spite of her more stable home situation, she rarely visited her children.

My heart broke every time I visited and my little friend looked up at me with his big brown eyes and told me that his mother hadn't been to see him since my last visit six months earlier.

Finally, the director of the orphanage gave me permission to contact the children's mother. I knew she was not working and didn't have an income, but I needed to know if there was any other reason why she was not visiting her children.

After much hunting, I got her telephone number and we arranged to meet at a coffee shop in Yerevan. I had no trouble identifying her when she arrived at the restaurant. Her son has her eyes totally. Over coffee, she explained that she had been sick. Thankfully, she laid my worst fear to rest— that her new husband might not want her children.

During our conversation, I wasn't getting a really good feeling, but, in spite of it, I offered to pay her transportation costs if she promised to visit her children at least once a month. She promised, and she said she would visit her children the very next day. The following evening, I called the orphanage and sure enough she had visited that day, and she told the director that she would be up from Yerevan on a regular basis. For a while she visited more regularly, and then she stopped.

Not long ago, I found out that she is planning to take them home to live with her soon. I feel very sad that the next time I'm in Armenia I may not see the little boy who has become my little angel, but it makes me happy to know that he's going home to live with his family and that our work at the orphanage has been successful.

Julie Ashekian, *Kensington, Connecticut*

The Art of Incensing

I love teaching the acolytes at our church. It's amazing how children absorb the faith and express it on their own terms in their own ways. Right now I have a six-year-old boy in my class, named Ethan, who is really enamored of holding candles and being in church.

Recently, his mother told me that when she and her son were shopping in the supermarket, he grabbed a bag of potatoes off the counter and began swinging it around. While swinging the potatoes, he accidentally hit a lady who was standing nearby. When his mother demanded to know what he thought he was doing, the young boy answered, "Mommy, this potato sack is my *pourvar* (censer). I'm practicing my sensing."

Ara Jeknavorian, *Chelmsford, Massachusetts*

A Sunday School Christmas Project

I don't think there is any better work than Christian education. I always get back ten times more than I give.

One year the Diocese asked the Sunday Schools to make and send ornaments to decorate the big Christmas tree in the cathedral in New York City. Our Sunday School decided to make oil-based painted glass ornaments. Every child did one, and they turned out beautifully. But, as we were finishing up, there was paint everywhere. I had paint all over me. The kids were running around like maniacs. Standing in the middle of the huge mess I thought, "Why do I do this to myself?"

As I was thinking that, one of the little girls came up to me, tugged on my skirt, and said, "Thank you, Ms. Lauren. This was so much fun."

Lauren Chalekian, *Racine, Wisconsin*

My Photographs

I started going to an Armenian church when they built one in my area of New Jersey. When the priest heard that I had a teaching background and had taught Sunday School in the Protestant church I had been attending, he asked me to help organize the Armenian Sunday School. Since then, I've taught Sunday School for more than fifty years, most of them at St. James Armenian Church in Watertown, Massachusetts, where I have been a parishioner since my marriage in 1956.

I have taken a lot of pictures over the years, and I believe in the power of photographs. I often send old pictures to people. Recently, a friend died. I wrote to his wife and sent her the pictures I had. She thanked me because the photographs I sent brought back a dear memory that was almost fifty years old.

Whenever I take a picture of a child, I make sure the child gets a copy so they can remember their past. Over the years, I have taught Sunday School to many children of students I had years before. They all seem to remember me—whether they listened to me or not.

One of the most important pictures I ever took was of the priest I met in New Jersey who initially asked me to help him all those years ago. Later, this priest became His Beatitude Archbishop Shnork Kaloustian, the Patriarch of Turkey. Since those early days, he has been my inspiration in the Armenian Church.

The last time I saw His Beatitude was in 1970, when my children were small. He came to my house and we shared a special dinner together. That day, we took pictures on the front lawn of our home. I placed one of them on the mantel in my living room next to a framed copy of the *Hayr Mer* (The Lord's Prayer).

Wherever His Beatitude went, he would remember my family and me with cards and letters, and I have saved them all. In my collection I have a letter written by him in 1988 telling me that he was going to Armenia to deliver a truck full of goods to the victims of the horrible earthquake. He died shortly after that trip. I had not seen him in many years, but his photograph was still on my mantel, and it still is. I look at it and remember him and his guidance and his friendship every day.

Irene Sarkisian, *Woburn, Massachusetts*

Serving Through the Kitchen

I am a Genocide survivor. I love my religion. I love my Lord Jesus Christ and his house of worship. I have been to many churches. They are all nice. Everybody does *Badarak*. But most of all I love the sunrise service at my church. Not many priests do it nowadays, but Father Mampre does it at Holy Trinity, and it inspires me.

I enjoy every morning that I am in church early. First, I hear Father Mampre. Then when he goes to be vested, I go to the hall and begin to put the *mas* (wafer) in the bags. Before, I used to make the *mas* with my friends, but they have all passed away, so I don't cook it any more, but I still put it in the bags. People arrive and come help me. We chat around. I love doing it.

I still cook for the bazaar. Last year, on Friday night alone, I cooked more than 120 pounds of rice. Saturday morning I just couldn't do it, so I asked for somebody to do the morning, and then in the afternoon I took over the kitchen again. Somehow the Lord gives me strength to do it.

I also have help. We have many lovely young ladies in our Women's Guild. They are all educated with degrees, but they are so humble and nice. They help you out. "Virgine, what can we do for you?" they ask.

Every year before Lent, Father Mampre always says, "Virgine, Lent is going to start. Why should you do all the cooking? Do two meals and let someone else do the others." I say, "I don't care. I'll cook as many meals as you want, but get someone to help with the shopping."

"Okay, we'll take care of that," he says.

That's how it is, and that's how I like it.

Virgine Kezarjian Mazmanian, *Arlington, Massachusetts*

A Behind-the-Scenes Look at a Funeral *Hokejash*

I'm in charge of the funeral *hokejash* dinners in our parish. Preparing a funeral *hokejash* is a two- to three-day job. I receive a call that someone has died and a *hokejash* has been requested. Once I know the date, I call the people on my team who always help set up the dining room. Those people call other people. I order the chicken and vegetables, place the bakery order, and do the grocery shopping. Then I take it all to the church.

On the day of the funeral, I arrive at the church at 7 o'clock in the morning. The rest of the ladies come at 8 o'clock or so. We make the salad and prepare the meal. It's important to have everything ready as soon as the family and mourners come back from the cemetery. We serve the meal, and we clean up afterwards.

I've been doing this for so long now and it goes so smoothly that sometimes I think I've forgotten to do something. I may be the one in charge, but it's not me, it's all about teamwork. I have a great team of volunteers, and we all work together.

People do not die for our convenience. Unless I have a doctor's appointment that I've waited months to get, everything is secondary to doing this job for my church community. I'm happy to do it for the families of the deceased, yet it's a sad occasion. Der Hayr says that it should be a happy time because the person who has passed is going on a journey, but it really isn't. Everybody is sad.

Pat Paragamian, *Racine, Wisconsin*

Taking the Church to Them

I am a member of the St. Gregory's Ladies Society, and I serve as the Chairperson for our Ladies Society Outreach Program in Fowler, California. Other women and I go to the private homes and nursing homes of parishioners who, either because of illness or age, can no longer come to church. Some people think that visiting the sick and the elderly is depressing, but it isn't. Everyone we visit is so happy when we arrive, you can see the sparkle in their eyes. We make their day, and it's a great feeling.

One lady I remember visiting was more than 100 years old. She's passed on since, but she told me that, in 1910, she was one of the first young girls to get married in our church. The church and chandelier were lit with candles in those days, and she laughed as she told me that, in the middle of the wedding ceremony, her Godmother's candle set her veil on fire. She ripped off her veil, crumbled it up, and threw it out the window. They went on with the wedding without missing a beat. I told that story to the rest of the members of our group, and everyone thought it was great.

On each visit, we try to bring home-baked *chorag* (tea bread) or some other Armenian food that they can no longer make or that isn't served where they are living. A few years ago, we got a cross-shaped baking mold from Armenia, and I made a batch of *chorag* in it. The *chorags* came out oddly shaped because *chorag* dough rises a lot, but they tasted fine, so we took them anyway. Everyone loved them, because they were different and special.

After each visit, we report back to the other members of our group as to how everyone is doing. If someone is eager to come to church but can't, we alert our priest, Father Kevork, so he can make a follow-up visit. I volunteer in other ways too, but bringing the church to those who can no longer attend is the most meaningful work I do for my parish.

Rose Samoulian, *Sanger, California*

Participating in the Holiday Folk Fair

I grew up in Milwaukee, Wisconsin. Every year, the city sponsored a very popular three-day holiday folk fair. More than fifty nationalities participated, and every year for well more than twenty years, our small church represented the Armenian nationality.

Everyone in the church was involved in making our booth one of the best food and cultural booths in the event. Our food was always very popular. We sold lamajun, sarma, boregs, and a variety of Armenian pastries. Believe it or not, our food sale revenue always ranked among the highest at the fair. We also worked hard to make sure that the cultural focus of our booth changed every year. One year we would focus on the Armenian alphabet; other years we would demonstrate the arts of Armenian crocheting, rug making, or cooking. Our church sponsored an Armenian folk dance group, which I was a member of, and we performed for large audiences twice a day throughout the weekend.

The fair ended about five years ago for our church community, but, for more than two decades, our little church made sure that the Armenians were a consistent presence. Even today, not many Armenians live in the Milwaukee area, and many people in the greater community are not familiar with Armenians, so our participation in the fair was a great opportunity for us to bring the Armenian culture to the Midwest.

Karen Durgarian, *Hopkinton, Massachusetts*

The Lesson of the Good Samaritan

As a child, I attended Holy Cross Armenian Church in New York City. On the mornings before Christmas and Easter, our pastor held a children's communion service. At these special services, he often told us the story of the Good Samaritan. The story is about a man robbing and beating another man and leaving him by the side of the road. A second man comes by, and, seeing the poor victim lying by the side of the road, he decides not to stop and help, believing that he has done nothing wrong by continuing his journey. Then a third man comes by. This man stops and helps the wounded man.

Even as a child, it was easy to understand that the man who had robbed and beaten another man had done wrong, but Hayr Sourp (Holy Father) explained to us that the second man was as great a sinner as the first man. The lesson of the story was that, as Christians, it is not enough for us to do no harm. Part of living a Christian life means helping other people whenever and wherever we see the need. This story had a profound effect upon me, and, although I don't consciously think of myself in the terms of being "a good Samaritan," the lesson of the story became part and parcel of my Christianity.

One likes to think that all of our service and involvement in the Armenian Christian community makes a difference. And I believe it does—often in small ways we don't see. But, after the 1988 earthquake in Armenia, I was blessed with the incredible opportunity of opening up my home to earthquake victims being airlifted to the greater New York–New Jersey area for medical treatment. With the consent and support of my family, we took these unfortunate victims into our home. Along with other members of a committee, we helped them receive the medical care they needed. I drove them to doctor appointments, to the hospital for surgery, and to the many physical therapy sessions they needed. It was a large commitment that required a lot of my time.

Recovery from the physical injuries and emotional battering these people experienced as trauma victims would have been difficult had they been in their own homes in Armenia, but here in the United States they had difficulty communicating with their care providers and experienced major culture shock.

My involvement with these earthquake victims had a dramatic and instant impact on their lives but it was not a one-way street. I used the word "blessed" because the lessons I learned about compassion, sharing, charity, kindness, sacrifice, and giving of one's self were far greater than any lesson I might have learned through sermons or lectures. It's hard to describe the joy and satisfaction I derived from helping the people I was able to help during that time. Several of them became like members of my family. Today, years later, the letters, pictures, and phone calls continue to flow between New Jersey and Armenia.

While in the throes of that experience, an acquaintance of mine took me aside one day and asked how I was able to do what I was doing. For a moment her question stopped me. Then I recalled the lesson of the Good Samaritan and I answered her question with a question of my own: "How can I not do what I am doing?"

Martha Saraydarian, *Englewood Cliffs, New Jersey*

A Little Girl's Service

My father is a priest. When I was a little girl, he often took me with him when he visited people in their homes. I remember visiting one woman in particular, because she had the cutest little dog named Coco who was about the same size I was at the time. I knew that it was my father's job to talk to people, but when we were at that woman's house, I thought my job was to play with the dog so he would not bother the adults while they were talking.

Talene Kelegian, *Racine, Wisconsin*

The Messenger

It was an October afternoon in Watervliet, New York. St. Peter Armenian Church sits at the top of a hill surrounded by forty acres of trees and bushes. Like a beacon, the church overlooks the Hudson River and the surrounding cities of Watervliet and Troy. That afternoon, I was meeting our Parish Council Chairman at the church. When he arrived, he told me that, as he was driving up the hill, he thought he saw something move in a dense section of trees along the road. It was a nice day, and he was curious, so he decided to walk down our drive and investigate.

He found a tent and a campsite-style living area in the thinning woods. Then, as he was standing there, a guy popped out of the tent. Our Parish Council Chairman screamed. The guy screamed. "What are you doing here?" they shouted at each other.

Our Chairman convinced the man to come with him up to the church. I was stunned when they walked into my office together. The man with our Chairman was about thirty-five years old, but he was really in rough shape; he was thin, his hair was wild, he had teeth missing, he wore ragged clothing, and he emitted a foul body odor. He was also armed with a BB gun.

At first he was kind of reserved, but we were able to discover that his name was Tony. We also found out that he had been living on the church property since August. At times during this early conversation, he would get a little aggressive. I think he was just scared. After repeated assurances that we would not hurt him, he finally turned over his gun.

Nothing like this had ever happened to me before. I had seen homeless people on the street, and I'd give them apples or some other food, but I had never contemplated inheriting a situation like this. The Parish Council Chairman and I knew we could not leave him on our property, but we really didn't know what to do, so we called the police.

The police arrived, and they, too, seemed kind of stunned. They searched him and scanned his name through their files. Thankfully he did not have a record. Once that was done, the police seemed to become indifferent. In contrast, I was feeling more and more called to deal with this situation. The Parish Council Chairman and I felt that somehow this homeless person was bringing us a message. It was then that we renamed him Gabriel.

The police suggested that we help Gabriel find a place in a shelter. We called around to some area shelters and found an opening in Albany. We told Gabriel that we would take him to the shelter. On the way there, we promised him that we would work with him and try to help him get back on his feet. He now had a church to support him. There were people like myself and other parishioners who would go downtown to the Social Services Department with him and make a plea on his behalf.

But, in spite of what we said, the closer to the shelter we got, the more nervous and paranoid Gabriel became. He told us that he had been there before, and to other shelters, and that this shelter was not safe. I discounted his words in my mind as we were driving, but when we walked into that shelter in Albany I too was scared. The facility was run down. It did not look safe or clean. Right away Gabriel said, "That's it, Father. I'm not staying here."

My wife and I discussed letting him stay at our house, but we really did not know him, and, while we wanted to be helpful and kind, we also needed to consider our own safety. We decided that he could stay in his tent on the church grounds since he'd been there for months and it wasn't terribly cold yet. A couple more nights would be okay, especially since we vowed to make sure that he'd receive help soon. Word got out, and members of our parish began bringing him hot meals and clothing. Over the next few days we raised enough money to get him a room in a hotel located near the church where he stayed for nearly a week. At that point, he was able to shower and get some rest. While Gabriel was at the hotel, it gave us an opportunity to work with him.

We started with Social Services in Albany. It was an eye-opening experience for me to witness firsthand what these people go through. It's easy to say, "Persevere. Go to Social Services. Everything will work out. I'll pray for you." That's not the case, and I found that out going with Gabriel. The employees looked down on him, they laughed at him, and they would not give him the time of the day. Had I not been there with my collar on, saying, "I'm his pastor. Listen to his case. We need to get him help. Let's work something out," he would not have been considered for assistance.

Social Services suggested that he be evaluated at the Psychological Evaluation Service office a few blocks away. That became our next step. Gabriel seemed agitated by the suggestion. We still didn't know how stable he was. He was showing signs of psychological distress—some of his stories weren't making sense, contradictions were becoming obvious and more frequent, and he was demonstrating signs of paranoia.

We found the Psychiatric Department and sat down in the waiting room. About a half-hour later, a counselor arrived to say that he could see Gabriel. They left together. When they returned, the counselor told us that he wanted to do some blood work. When Gabriel heard that, he became really nervous and said he wanted to leave. We tried to convince him that he should stay and have the work done because it would be helpful, but, in mid-conversation, Gabriel jumped up and ran from the unit. Worse than his leaving, the counselor told us that during their interview, Gabriel had said something threatening to him.

When that happens it's policy to consider the patient a potential harm to society. They must have him arrested and brought to the hospital for a mental health evaluation.

In a matter of minutes, Gabriel had threatened the counselor and bolted from the clinic. A police search was initiated because of what he had said to the counselor. He was on the loose, and either the police or we had to find him on the streets of Albany. At that point, we were having second thoughts about our involvement with him. Quite honestly, we were not sure what we had gotten ourselves into.

But finding him seemed like the best course of action, so we got in the car and began looking. We found him about a half a mile from the clinic. Now he was cautious of us, wondering what we were going to make him do. We begged him to get in the car and to talk things through. Finally, he did. We promised him again and again that whatever he had to do we would stick by him every step of the way.

I guess he must have felt that trust, because finally he agreed. We took him to the Albany Medical Center Crisis Unit. It was either there or the police station—there was no other choice. At the Albany Medical Center, we had another eye-opening experience. In all fairness, the crisis unit people said that they had not seen a night like that in twelve years.

We arrived at 7:00 p.m. and did not leave until 4:00 a.m. the following morning. The last person Gabriel met before he was admitted called us in for a group meeting. He suggested that Gabriel have a full physical and emotional evaluation. The doctors told us that they could diagnose Gabriel's medical condition and prescribe treatment, and then they could advise Social Services how best to address Gabriel's needs and concerns.

We agreed to that plan. Over the next ten days, during his evaluation period, we met with some very nice doctors. We discovered that Gabriel's parents had been killed in an explosion that also destroyed the family home years before. He had not been in the house at the time of the explosion, but he was scarred emotionally from that event. He had some physical problems, and there were also some chemical imbalances in his body that a regular regimen of medications could address.

The good news was that Gabriel was finally receiving care and being plugged into the New York Social Services System.

When he was released from the hospital, Gabriel went straight into an apartment we found for him. We raised the first few month's rent, security deposit, and some furniture money from within the community. He still lives in that apartment.

Gabriel came to church a few Sundays after that, and he began giving us gifts. These were things he found on the street, but they were his possessions. He gave angels to all the people in the parish who had helped him out.

A short time later, one Sunday, the Bishop was visiting and during the procession he blessed Gabriel, who was very excited about that. "The Bishop blessed me today," he said. Those Sunday visits gave us, as a parish, a chance to meet with him and wish him well.

People continued to bring him meals and check up on him throughout the next year. Our Parish Council Chairman and his wife made it their personal responsibility to follow up with him to make sure he was taking his medications and that things were okay. We got him a job at McDonald's, and he worked for a while, but at a certain point he was making too much money, and the state threatened to take him off disability. That created a problem for him, and I don't believe he's currently working.

At first, we tried to help change some of Gabriel's personality traits and habits, but we realized there was no way we could do that. He's a strange person. He likes to go out at night. He's famous for riding his bike throughout town at night and for picking up scrap metal. To this day, if I'm driving home late from the church and I see his bike, I stop and chat with him and assure him that we are still here for him.

What helped Gabriel was a community that supported him and showed him love and mercy. Most importantly, we interceded for him. Who would have done that for him before our finding him camped on our property? Perhaps no one.

We learned that we could not change him, but we could positively affect his condition and environment.

His experience with us changed his perspective of the church and of God as well. Another church in town sponsors a soup kitchen, and Gabriel goes there every Wednesday night. They love him. I speak to that pastor every couple of months, and he always tells me how great Gabriel is doing. Our church helps out at the soup kitchen from time to time, and we see him there too. So, he's found that community as well. He now has an extended family.

As we went through this experience, we prayed and felt God directing him and us. You never know when God is going to present you with an opportunity to act and to live out your faith. I'm happy to say that, when Gabriel walked in our door, our community showed their Christian spirit. Whenever we talk about Gabriel in our parish, people smile.

> Reverend Father Stepanos Doudoukjian, *Latham, New York*

BEING THERE FOR PEOPLE IS PART OF THE JOB

One day, the son of a very dear friend of mine, a young man who had also served with me at the altar, called to ask if I was going to be in the office for a while and could wait until he got there. "It's important," he said. It was a nice day, so I waited for him in the parking lot. The minute he arrived and got out of the car, I could see that something was bothering him. We embraced and he began to sob.

"Der Hayr," he said, "I have to tell somebody. I'm addicted to cocaine. I'm an addict. I've tried to shake it, and I can't. Please, can you help me?"

With my help and the support of his family, he got himself into a recovery program and began working through his condition. The marriage he was in at the time did not survive, but a decade later, he's still sober. I don't know how much of a difference I made by being there for him, but the idea that I was there and he felt he could come to me and I would keep his confidence—it was a very humbling experience.

He and I were always close, but, as a result of that experience, we have grown even closer. I think a lot of times people are afraid that if they get too close to their priest it's going to damage something. My experience has been the opposite.

> Reverend Father Vartan Kasparian, *Visalia, California*

A Tax Collector's Perspective

I've been with the Internal Revenue Service since 1967 as a Revenue Agent. During Lent, when we talk about the tax collector, people always point a finger at me. Over the years, I've left many a tax audit blessing the people for what they have done. I've seen firsthand how generous people can be in their financial support of their churches and other charitable institutions. Our faith teaches us to tithe to the church, and our churches and institutions depend on this support. It's important for all of us to share a part of our wealth with the community.

Deacon Allan Y. Jendian, *Fresno, California*

Who Gives What

Traditionally, in our parish, when a person died, the donations given by parishioners were printed in the church bulletin by family name followed by the amount of money the family gave. When my husband died, I refused to conform to this tradition. Instead, I insisted that my husband's memorial gifts be listed in the bulletin alphabetically by last name with the total amount given in his memory reported at the end.

Our priest at the time resisted this change in procedure. He said, "That's the only way you get money in this church."

But I believe that if we give and feed the people with what they need to be fed with—that you accept Jesus Christ in your life and live your life according to His word—the money will come. People will give because they are receiving what they are seeking, not because the Santerians gave so much money so the Asadoorians will give at least as much or more. We no longer do that in our parish. Thank God!

Merle Santerian, *Huntingdon Valley, Pennsylvania*

An Odd Rule

If you look at our church calendar, there are activities and services every day, but, at least in the 21st century in the West, the high point of the communal Christian week is attending services together on Sunday. One of the sad realities of attending the Divine Liturgy is that many of our community do not attend, and many of those who do attend are not in the sanctuary. They are outside talking, smoking, or enjoying breakfast at a restaurant down the street. Or they are in an office somewhere. Go to any Armenian Church and any parish council room during *Badarak* and you are going to see parish council people in it, talking and counting money. So, even in the Sunday *Badarak,* we don't have participation in the *Badarak*. We can't do much about the people who stay home on any given Sunday, but we can do something about the people who are physically in the environment of the church—either outside, down the street, or in an office.

When I served as Treasurer for our parish, I made a new rule. My rule was that if you wanted to see the Treasurer, if you wanted to make a donation, if you wanted something in the bulletin, you had to see me either before *Badarak* or after *Badarak*, because during *Badarak* I was in church. Right away someone approached me in church needing to make a donation. I told them that they would have to wait until after the service. Then, during coffee hour, someone asked me how come I wasn't in the parish council room during church, because he wanted something in next week's bulletin. After a couple of weeks, people figured it out.

The message to the congregation was, "I am in church. You have no excuse not to be in church." Through my action, I told people that the most important thing I do on Sunday is not count the money, it's participating in the service with my community. Action by example has a trickle-down effect. People saw what I was doing and followed my lead. It was a small thing, really, but for me it was a very important decision.

Charlie Shooshan, *Newington, Connecticut*

No Limelight for Me

I do what I need to do. I work, help out, guide, be there, whatever, but I don't like the focus to come back on me. I prefer to do things quietly, because that's the way I think Jesus was.

Anonymous, *Fresno, California*

The Armenian Church's Place in the World

The Armenian Church is generally considered to be a national church. But I think that this idea of a national church—a church devoted to a people, which is after all what a nation means—has been misunderstood. Lately, we have conflated nationhood with the idea of the state. But a nation is not necessarily a state; think of the American Indian nations, for example. A nation is made up of its natives—a group of people who have a common heritage, language, and some shared historical experience.

When you think about it, a church devoting itself to a particular people is a humble idea.

The Christian religion itself is a universal idea. God created all of the universe, and His son saved the sins of all mankind. All nations and people are to be evangelized. But, for some reason, the Armenians felt that it was enough to focus attention on the people they know and have some real relationship with. In this regard, maybe we were the first to have this insight, and maybe it is one of the things we should feel proudest about as Armenian Christians.

In affirming this idea, we are rejecting a kind of universalism that is usually phony and all too easy. It's easy to say you love "humanity," that you love people living on the other side of the world. But that is an abstraction. I will go so far as to say that any person who says such a thing is a liar. All you have to do is go to the supermarket and stand in line for half an hour to recognize what a lie it is. You look at the crowd of people around you, and the cashier, and all you can think is how much you can't stand them—and you don't even know them. So much for loving "humanity." But to say you love your countrymen—there is some reality to that statement of love. Your countrymen are people who in some sense you are capable of loving in a substantial way.

There is a quality of humility to the idea of a national church that is impressive and beautiful to me. In a way, its opposite may be seen in the Roman Catholic church, which makes a passive or explicit claim to be the universal church—the single, authoritative church of Christ's teaching on earth. This imperial attitude is quite attractive, but it has also resulted in terrible, terrible injustices, like the Crusades and the Inquisition—things that the Roman Catholic church is still paying a price for in terms of the way the rest of the world looks upon it and, more importantly, in terms of the credibility of the message of love that it seeks to propagate.

Also standing in opposition to the national church is the Protestant idea, which embodies a different kind of universalism. It's just you and the Man Upstairs; that's the critical dynamic. Each individual person is on his own little wavelength with God, and institutions like nations and, for that matter, churches really don't mean much. But this too has its worst-case scenario. This type of universalism has a tendency to become more and more elastic and less and less tied to any coherent set of beliefs. The result, on the one hand, can be the flaccid and even vacuous feel-goodism seen in today's mainline Protestantism; on the other hand, the reaction can be a sort of fundamentalism that, however interesting, its reflections on Scripture tends towards a kind of "text idolatry" that makes the inner truth of the religion seem banal.

The Armenian Church may offer a way to walk between these poles—to walk humbly in the path of God. Maybe our church represents a midpoint between the imperial church, which can be oppressive, and the believing individual, who in the plainest sense is without support and lonely. We don't have to assume that there is anything earth-shaking about our church. Being a national church is not about waving the flag as an exclusivist organization, or about making statements like, "It's our church and it's the greatest." Rather, maybe the character of the Armenian Church is a realistic reflection on the possibility of evangelization. Maybe it is a meditation in humility about what the limits of evangelization can be, and perhaps ought to be.

Because our church is a national church, it does not assume the one-size-fits-all idea of Christianity. At the same time, it reaches out to more than just the individual. It reaches out to the community of people who share a certain background, a certain historical experience, a certain language. It understands that we are not the only game in town and that the people next door to us also have a duty to take care of their own. We can be fraternal, love each other, expect to benefit from each other, but, as far as our ultimate obligation goes, it's enough for us to say that we can take care of our own backyard and not to say that we are going to take over the whole world—and in doing so, perhaps, terrorize the world, or lose our backyard.

Christopher Zakian, *New York, New York*

The Encyclopedia of Religion

I was fortunate to have had the opportunity to work on the editorial committee involved in the publication of a comprehensive, multi-volume work published by Macmillan Publishing entitled *The Encyclopedia of Religion*. Technically, I was in charge of the Islam and Judaic sections, but during a general editorial meeting I noticed that, in the section on Christianity, only one article had been assigned to Eastern Orthodoxy, which included the Byzantine Orthodox and the Oriental Orthodox churches. Given such little coverage, I feared that Orthodoxy in general would not be well represented and that the Oriental Orthodox churches would hardly receive a mention. I brought up my concern, and my colleagues listened. We spoke to our supervisor and then to the editor of the Christianity section, who was a Catholic priest.

Raising our concerns changed everything. As a result, an introductory article was allocated to Eastern Christianity, and individual articles were devoted to each of the Orthodox churches, including the Armenian Church. In addition, each jurisdiction received a minimum of five short articles devoted to the lives of important people in these churches' traditions, and the Eastern Orthodox perspective was included in the thematic articles that were originally going to present only the Catholic and Protestant perspectives.

By being involved at the editorial level, I was able to influence the treatment that Orthodoxy received in a very authoritative work.

Yeretzgin Sirarpi Feredjian Aivazian, *Fresno, California*

The Gathering of Christians

For eight years, I served as a member of a delegation chosen to represent the Diocese of the Armenian Church of America (Eastern) at annual meetings of the National Council of the Churches of Christ. My first experience as a delegate was in Texas. It was the first time that I was exposed to all of the different churches—Episcopal, Lutheran, Methodist—and the variety amazed me.

At the convention, all the delegates from the different churches worshiped and shared a traditional Christian sacrament together at a special gathering called the Gathering of Christians. That first year, I remember that we broke bread together. We each received the sacrament, and then we held hands and sang a song. I had never experienced anything like that before, and I felt that I had been given a great opportunity just to be there.

Right after the earthquake in Armenia, I mounted photographs of the earthquake area and its victims on poster board and displayed them in the lobby of the hotel where we were meeting that year. You have to realize that the delegates were from all over the United States, and many of them come to the meeting without ever having heard of Armenians or the Armenian Church. So many people stopped to look at the photos that I have photos of people looking at the photos.

I also learned quickly that most of the churches have the utmost respect for the Armenian Apostolic Church and for our hierarchy.

Julie Ashekian, *Kensington, Connecticut*

Our World Reputation

I have traveled a great deal for business. Wherever I am in the world—Shanghai, Dubai, Latin America—I have found that people have a great respect for Armenians. I won't say it's strictly religion. They know we are Christian, but it is also who we are in terms of the world community.

One time, my business took me to the middle of the Saudi Arabian desert, where I hoped to help solve a land problem. The land needed to be demarcated, and the Muslim Sheiks involved were having a tough time deciding what would be fair. After much discussion, they were still unable to arrive at a satisfactory solution. Finally, they turned to me. "The Armenian has integrity," they said. "Let him decide how the land should be divided."

I took a stick and drew two lines in the desert sand. Both lines were straight except for two half-circle, bubble-shapes. The half-circle shaped sections of the boundary lines preserved the water rights of each side involved. By protecting each Sheik's right to access the traditional water wells used by their sheep and camel herds, I was able to suggest a solution to the problem that was seen as fair and that was accepted. I'm not certain the problem would have been as easy to solve had the Sheiks not been able to trust "the Armenian's integrity."

As Armenians, we have a responsibility that extends beyond the United States or the community where we grew up. The world community knows who we are, and people have great expectations of us. I am really proud of that. There is always a sleaze factor in every ethnic community, and we are no different. We have that small percentage, but, for the most part, anywhere I have been in the world, I have been proud to be an Armenian, and I have been treated with respect. We are a unique people. But I have found that with that uniqueness comes a responsibility that goes beyond yourself.

Carl Bazarian, *Amelia Island, Florida*

Go Back to the Church of Your Ancestors

I grew up in the Armenian Church, but in college an Episcopal bishop whose father had been a missionary in Armenia took me under his wing, and I began to consider becoming an Episcopal priest. Before I made any decisions with regard to my future, my mentor asked me to visit churches other than the Armenian and Episcopal parishes I knew. When the time came for me to make my decision, he told me that he had asked me to visit other churches for two reasons: first, to improve my spirit, and second, to show me some of the good things that were being done by other Christian faiths that could be done in the Armenian Church as well. Then he said, "Now, go back to the church of your ancestors. There's a great tradition there, and that tradition has been injured."

The Armenian Church is an injured church. It was injured while trying to survive 500 years of Ottoman domination. It survived, but that survival meant accommodating in some way—assimilating, hiding, and deceiving. As if that had not been damaging enough, the church and our people then suffered Genocide. The majority of our great churchmen were killed during the massacres. After the war, the few who survived either gathered in Jerusalem to revitalize the Seminary of Jerusalem or went to Lebanon to rebuild the Seminary of Antilias out of the rubble.

They did their best to train priests to serve the people, but this was all done under very trying circumstances. Many of the young men who entered the seminaries in the early days after the massacres were orphans. They had been injured psychologically and emotionally by the traumas they had endured. So, even with the best of training, they would not have left, nor did they leave, our seminaries as perfect products. The same was true of many of our parishioners. They were survivors who had fled their homes under the threat of annihilation. As recent immigrants to the various countries in which they found themselves after the massacres, many worked at dirty, hard jobs.

One of the only ways they could fulfill the human need for status and prestige and recognition within the community was by serving the church in offices like the parish council. Holding positions of leadership in the church meant success to them. But, like the priests who had been traumatized and trained in our post-Genocide seminaries, so suffered many of our laymen involved in the church. We can see a lot of problems in our church originating from that difficult history.

I did not leave our church, but I was ready to leave it. Instead, I accepted the wise advice of my mentor. I've spent my life trying to serve my church as best I can, and I think we've made tremendous progress. One small example is that, in the old days, at the annual meeting of the Diocesan Assembly, people would yell and scream at each other. When I was chairman, I introduced Parliamentary procedure. People began to treat each other in a courteous manner that continues to this day.

Armenians can set the Armenian Church aright if we do come back and work towards making a contribution. If we don't come back and serve our church, then our church will atrophy.

Dr. Dennis R. Papazian, *Troy, Michigan*

Vow of Silence

I am an Armenian-American. The only grandparents I knew were on my father's side. My grandmother survived the massacres and came to the United States as a house girl for a Presbyterian minister and his family. My grandfather migrated to the United States in 1895, so he missed a lot of the massacres, but both ended up with hardly any family alive after World War I. My grandparents never talked about their past. It was if they had taken a vow of silence. If they needed to talk about anything bad, they spoke in Turkish so that no one could understand them.

When my father got married and had his own family, he didn't talk about anything bad either. So I grew up knowing absolutely nothing about my ancestors. Like the majority of Armenians in America during that time, my grandparents and my parents wanted us to be Americans. We were not given Armenian names. There were no Arams or Sarkises at Armenian summer camp when I was a camper. We all had American names like Jack, Paul, and Diane.

Every time I participated in anything Armenian, I did so consciously. I made a conscious choice to go to Armenian summer camp instead of the YMCA camp. In college, I chose to take Armenian studies, to join the Armenian Students' Organization, and to participate in Armenian Church Youth Organization (ACYO) activities. I met my husband at an ACYO event, and, in 1977, I took a trip to Armenia with the ACYO to visit Etchmiadzin and the other churches there. That was when I began to get a sense of how impressive our history is, especially our Christian history.

For me, remaining Armenian has been a constant choice and effort, and I'm not sure why I do it. My father is gone. My mother does not go to the Armenian Church much. My brother has totally fallen away. For me, the church has been the one constant, unchanging Armenian force in my life. I don't know what made me keep pushing until I broke through the wall of silence about my heritage, but I'm glad I did.

Paulette Kalebjian, *Fresno, California*

No Longer Pinching Myself

I grew up in the Armenian Church. My earliest recollections revolve around the church. The feasts and the fasts were part my family's tradition and the way we lived our lives. So I was always attending church.

Along about my teen years, I began to feel that this was something very special, and I began to ask if there was some way that I could give my life in service. In 1963, when I was a senior in high school, St. Nersess Seminary was just getting off the ground in Evanston, Illinois. The church held its first summer conference in Evanston that summer. A number of idealistic young people like me attended that first conference. We talked about how we could serve the church. Ordination was not on the radar screen for women, but several of the young men who attended that first conference went on to be ordained, and they continue to serve the Armenian Church as priests today. It was a very vital event and time for many of us.

It was the 1960s, and the whole world was changing. Archbishop Tiran, who was the driving force behind the concept of a seminary in the United States, also could see a role for women in lay ministry in the church. He talked about women becoming directors of religious education and youth workers—if they got the theological education and training. This appealed to me.

I went to college and received my undergraduate degree. Then, in the summer of 1968, I represented the orthodox Christian youth as a delegate to the World Council of Churches Assembly in Sweden. On my way back from Sweden, I stopped in New York City to attend an Armenian Church Youth Organization Central Council meeting. The Primate pulled me aside. "Whatever happened to you going to seminary?" he asked. Four weeks later, I was enrolled in Seabury Western, the Episcopal Seminary that St. Nersess was affiliated with in Evanston.

I was young and idealistic and full of enthusiasm. I was one of a few women studying at the seminary and the only non-Episcopalian woman. The Episcopal Church was not ordaining women then, either. I graduated with an M.A. in 1970.

For the next three years, I worked at the Diocese in New York directing the department of Religious Education. While at the Diocese, I married and had my first child. In 1976, the church in Tenafly, New Jersey, offered me the chance to be their religious education person on a part-time basis. This seemed perfect. By then I had two children, so part-time was about all I could manage. I did that for a number of years. But, toward the late 1970s, a feeling, an urge, an urgency about ordination started to grow within me. By that time, the Episcopal Church was ordaining women as priests.

I kept going back to the scripture and looking at the radical changes the Gospel had brought to people's lives. In particular, I was drawn to the lesson Peter learned in Acts.

Originally, he thought the Gospel message was only to be delivered to the Jews. Finally, he came to understand that the Gospel was supposed to go beyond the narrow parameters that he had put around it. Ultimately, Peter took the Gospel to Rome, the most important city of the known world. I figured that, if the Gospel and the love of Jesus Christ and the Good News is meant for all people, then, surely, like Peter, the Armenian Church could go beyond the narrow understanding it had of ordination. Times were different. The church was crying out for people to serve it, and the Armenian Church had a tradition of woman deacons. They were cloistered nuns, but they were still full deacons.

Why couldn't I be ordained as a deacon and in doing so fulfill the calling I felt growing within me?

I was less young but still idealistic. I began publicly writing and talking about it. Then, in 1982, I was invited to deliver a paper on the ordination of women as deacons to the Diocesan Assembly, which I did. Some people were offended, and a few priests walked out of the hall, but, in general, it was received politely. Four years later, a number of people raised the issue again. The 1986 Diocesan Assembly overwhelmingly approved the resolution for women being ordained as deacons in the United States, and they asked the Primate to take the initiative to Etchmiadzin.

At that time, I was working with Father Arnak Kasparian in Tenafly as a pastoral assistant. In hindsight, I realize now that he gave me enough rope to hang myself. I spent the next three to four years doing pastoral ministry. I visited the sick in the hospital. I prepared people for baptism. I did some administrative jobs in the parish office. But I could not preach. I could not celebrate the sacraments, including the *Badarak*, of course. Many of the parishioners received me with warm, open arms; others were bothered. It was new and different. I was charting new territory.

As I served the Tenafly community, I tried to figure out what I was being called to do. This call, this pull, this urgency to serve kept growing. I could visit someone in the hospital, but I could not take him communion.

Those kinds of things were hard. I was still hopeful that the Diocese was going to proceed with its plans to ordain women as deacons, but the leadership had changed, and it became clearer and clearer that the ordination of women to the diaconate, never mind the priesthood, was not a current possibility in the Armenian Church.

I grew older and less idealistic. I began thinking, "Is there life outside the Armenian Church?" At first I could not imagine it, but, in 1991, when Father Arnak retired, I left the Armenian Church and began pursuing ordination in the Episcopal Church. Today I serve the Episcopal Church as a priest in my parish in Stamford, Connecticut.

I'm no longer pinching myself, but, for the longest time, I did. Leaving the Armenian Church was the hardest thing I had done in my life. I felt like I was being divorced from my family. But it was also what I needed to do and what God was calling me to do. On one hand, I'm still sorry that this is how it had to happen. On the other hand, I know it could not have been otherwise. The Armenian Church could not ordain me, but my journey was a long, hard, very painful struggle.

You can take me out of the Armenian Church, but you can't take the Armenian Church out of me. It's the tradition that taught me the Gospel and that nurtured me. I am grateful that I am able to share the Armenian Christian heritage with other people through my ministry as an Episcopal priest, and I hope that I can still serve the Armenian Church in one way or another in the years to come, as opportunities arise. My decision to leave was the only option for me; I don't advocate it for others unless God's insistent call leaves no other choice.

The Reverend Louise Kalemkerian, *Stamford, Connecticut*

The Lesson of the Prodigal Son

I discovered my Armenian Christian while heritage sitting in a Catholic church at Boston College. It happened that way, first, because of the English language used in the Catholic mass; and, second, because at Boston College there were teachers teaching about Christianity. One night while attending a midnight mass on campus, it dawned on me that what they were doing and saying was the same as in the Armenian Church.

I was brought up in St. James Armenian Church in Watertown, Massachusetts. Even though I had an excellent spiritual leader, there were formidable barriers to participating in the service at St. James. It's possible that, at that point in my life, even if the Liturgy had been delivered in English, it may have not made a difference, so, while leaving that possibility open, the reality for me was that I came to faith in another church—or, at least, independent of the Armenian Church. Then, once my faith was awakened, I discovered and embraced the Armenian Apostolic church.

One of my favorite stories in the Bible is the story of the Prodigal Son. The Prodigal Son leaves his home and, when he returns, he loves his father more intensely than the son who stayed at home does. In part, the Prodigal Son appreciates his father more after seeing the evils of the world, but I think the greater lesson is that, only after going away and returning home is the son's love for the father a free choice.

Often, no matter who you are, the religion you grew up with isn't a free choice. To a certain extent, it's forced upon you, and, at some level, at some time, whatever faith you chose needs to be appropriated as your own. Sometimes you have to leave to come back. Sometimes, too, this part of the spiritual journey is seen as a threat in our church, but I see it as a necessity, and part of the challenge we all face on our journeys.

Jason Demerjian, *Waltham, Massachusetts*

Divided We Fall

I have explored other disciplines of Christianity. I grew up in the Armenian Church, but in college I was active in on-campus Evangelical Protestant groups. The reason I came back to the Armenian Church was two-fold. First, it has sustained our people for more than 1700 years through unbelievable adversity. William Saroyan wrote, "Go ahead. Try to destroy these people." I believe the reason we have persevered against seemingly insurmountable odds is because of Christ's guidance.

The other reason I returned to the orthodox Armenian faith is that, once I examined all aspects of the Protestant Evangelical born-again religion, I realized that there was no reason to leave our church, because everything is there. For instance, a common criticism of our church is that we are not biblically based. People say that our church hierarchy developed the *Badarak* based on their interpretations of the Gospel rather than the Gospel itself, but that is not true. Not only is the Divine Liturgy biblically based, but our church calendar of readings also covers the Bible on an annual basis.

Then there is our practice of infant baptism that combines three sacraments—Baptism (*Mgrdootiun*), Christening (*Troshm*), and Holy Communion (*Soorp Haghortootiun*). The Protestant-based religions tend to reject the idea of infant confirmation, saying that an individual must make a personal choice. On one level, I agree with them. I believe there comes a time in every person's journey of faith when the decision to accept Jesus Christ needs to be made, but I do not believe that the two are mutually exclusive. In orthodoxy, when we bring a child into the church, we are bringing them into God's family. Why would you not want to bring that child into God's family at the earliest possible moment?

I think we could benefit from following the example practiced by the Protestants of having a separate confirmation or age of accountability ceremony. Since our church doesn't do that, I try to address the issue in my Sunday School classes. I tell my students that their parents have given them this start in life, but at some point they must be prepared to stand up and say that Jesus Christ is their personal Lord and Savior.

Maybe it's because I have practiced my faith from both the Protestant and Orthodox perspectives, but it bothers me when people, non-believers and believers alike, try to find divisions and reasons to separate one Christian believer from another. Maybe the Catholics give a greater role to the Virgin Mary, and maybe in Orthodoxy we like to picture the risen Christ, and maybe the Protestants prefer to emphasize the crucifixion, but in the end we are all saying and believing in the same components. When people try to divide us, they are playing into Satan's hands. That is a very bad thing, and we must not allow it to happen.

Nick Kazarian, *Fresno, California*

A Matter of Comfort

I was the first baby baptized in the Holy Cross Church of Armenia in New York City when it opened in 1928. However, I've always felt that that distinction was more a matter of good timing than anything else. I belong to the church. I'm part of it, it's part of me, although I've never had a revelation. There's been no singular spiritual or religious event that turned my life around. I don't attend regularly. My parents didn't either. But I never felt that I was not in good standing. Over the years I've felt proud of and comfortable with my church.

Edgar Housepian, M.D., *New York, New York*

Everything Worthwhile Takes Effort

Some people are like corks floating in the river, going where the currents take them. Do you want to be a cork? Who wants to drift in the river? I don't. I want to determine my life. I want to decide what I want to do. What I want to be. And being an Armenian Christian is a part of that. It's about not just taking the easy way. It takes effort to be a violinist. It takes effort to be a painter or a writer. It takes effort to be an Armenian Christian. Everything worthwhile takes effort.

Dr. Dennis R. Papazian, *Troy, Michigan*

Tradition Smiled on Me

One unusual time that I felt I was in touch with the church's greatness and beauty was when I was sick. I had gone through the regimen of chemotherapy once. The cancer came back, so I had to go through a second, more rigorous regimen that included radiation and a month-long hospital stay. Oddly, during that second treatment period, although I had a few melancholy days, I was confident I could endure the treatment.

A day or two before I was to be discharged from the hospital, Archbishop Barsamian and Father Krikor Maksoudian came to visit me. My wife was there in the room. I had lost my hair and was thinner than normal, but I was glad to have been disconnected from the I.V. We chatted a little bit, then they decided to say a prayer. Dressed in their black street attire, the two priests stood at the foot of my bed and began praying in *krapar*, the medieval Armenian dialect still used in the church. That was the first time that I really got choked up.

The prayer was like a doorway. The Armenian language and the sterile hospital room were at total odds with each other. The words of the prayer were the same words that have been spoken for centuries, and now they were being said over me. They seemed to symbolize the richness of the world—of an outside world that I had been apart from for a month, of a world that reached back more than eighty-five generations and that would likely reach forward for as many. At that moment, as I witnessed those two opposites—the sparse efficiency of the hospital room side by side with the elegant ritual of that ancient prayer spoken in those ancient words—the *krapar* won. It was escorting me back into the world of the living.

I thought, "I'm going home in a couple of days." My hair is going to grow back, and I'm going to get on with my life.

Christopher Zakian, *New York, New York*

Old Book of Prayers

In our church we have an old book of prayers called a *zhamakirk* in Armenian. It was published in Jerusalem in 1890. Its pages are fragile, so I don't use it often. During morning services when I do use it, I always wonder about the journey the book has taken, through four or five generations of deacons and altar servers, to arrive in my church. How many hands have held it before mine?

Singing the ancient hymns from that book never fails to inspire an emotional and spiritual response within me. It's a very special feeling I only get when I'm in church and allowed, as a deacon, the privilege of using such a sacred object of our faith.

Ara Jeknavorian, *Chelmsford, Massachusetts*

Good Turk, Bad Turk

Armenian Christianity needs to focus on forgiveness. As a people, we have a significant issue with the Turks. Maybe my upbringing was unique, but I grew up in an Armenian home that was both Armenian-speaking and Turkish-speaking. My father's side of the family spoke Armenian. My mother's side spoke Turkish. Many of my Turkish-speaking relatives were intimate with what took place during the 1915 Genocide. Often, they ended their stories of how they escaped deportation by saying, "I would not be here if there were not good Turks." When I was a child, they made sure I understood that there were bad Turks and there were good Turks.

In contrast, my father's side of the family spoke only about bad Turks. Although no one on that side of the family had actually witnessed any of the atrocities, they were very staunch about their perception of Turkish people.

Then my Armenian-speaking father went into business with my Turkish-speaking grandmother. Together they operated a successful little delicatessen in Indian Orchard, Massachusetts. Through the business, my grandmother found and made friends with a Turkish doctor who had immigrated to the United States and was living nearby. At the time he was working in an institution, but he did not have his medical certification. My grandmother introduced him to her sister who suffered from a debilitating form of epilepsy. This Turkish doctor was the first one who worked with my great-aunt and who actually helped improve her condition. Under his care, she stabilized and became able to hold down a job.

My father was so impressed with the work this doctor did for my great-aunt that he welcomed him into our home and interceded on his behalf to get him his papers so he could live and practice medicine in this country.

We have an immense ability to forgive and to overcome our prejudices. My father learned to treat that Turkish doctor as an individual rather than to politicize his relationship based on why Turks and Armenians should hate each other.

Today, when I meet a Turk, what am I supposed to do, ask them if their ancestors were good Turks or bad Turks? If my family is any example, a lot of Armenians would not be in this country or have had the opportunities they had in life if some Turks not risked their own lives to hide them from the murderous perpetrators of atrocities.

Karnig Durgarian, *Hopkinton, Massachusetts*

Open Your Eyes to the Truth

In 1995, on the 80th Anniversary of the Genocide, the Commonwealth of Massachusetts honored me as a survivor. I got a telephone call from people at the State House. They said that they were looking for somebody who was born in Anatolia, because the Armenians living in the Eastern provinces of the Ottoman Empire suffered the worst tortures and there were hardly any survivors.

"I am from Anatolia section," I said. "But I am not going to tell you my birthplace, because I may have relatives still in Turkey, and they will torture them."

"That's fine," they said.

At the State House in downtown Boston, I was introduced to Governor Weld and Paul Celluci, who was Lieutenant Governor at that time. "Where's the walker? The wheelchair? The cane?" Governor Weld asked me.

"What are you talking about? None of that so far," I said.

"What is the recipe?" he asked.

"Good old-fashioned hard work—the Armenian way."

That day, I got so much pleasure marching under the United States flag and the Armenian flag. Then, while I was sitting on the podium waiting to be introduced, I whispered to a friend, "Tell me. All these people come and every year someone is honored. What do the people say?"

"They say thank you and that's it," he said.

After the Lieutenant Governor introduced me, I asked if I could say a few words. I stood on that podium and I told the crowd gathered in front of me that the war in Karabagh was not a civil war but a war for religious freedom. I told them that our Armenian boys were fighting and dying for their religion as well as their homeland.

"Please Elected Officials," I said. "Open your eyes to the truth."

Virgine Kezarjian Mazmanian, *Arlington, Massachusetts*

April 24

When I was the Commander of the Ararat Lodge of the Knights of Vartan, Father Dajad Davidian called me up to tell me that the gentleman who organized the April 24 ceremony at the Boston State House every year was retiring. He suggested that the Knights of Vartan pick up the banner for that event.

I agreed to take the project on, and I contacted all the other Armenian organizations in town. I was able to get them to agree that the Commemoration of the Genocide was not a religious or a political event, but that it was important to the Armenian community as a whole. For the first time, all the organizations came through and decided to support the Knights of Vartan as the neutral organization best suited to sponsor the event. Ararat Lodge gave due recognition to all who participated, and this level of cooperation among the different Armenian groups in Boston continues to this day. I am very happy about that achievement.

Haig Deranian, *Belmont, Massachusetts*

Becoming Adults

The longer we are here in America, the less important the nationality part of the Armenian Christian equation becomes. I married a non-Armenian, and I am witness to the continued assimilation of my own children and grandkids. My three children know they have an Armenian heritage, and, during their younger years, they learned some of the folk dances and to read and write a little bit. To celebrate their becoming adults, I gave them a copy of *The Forty Days of Musa Dagh,* and an Armenian cookbook when they turned twenty-one. While I have yet to be invited to any of their homes for an Armenian meal, I'm still hoping. They know they are Armenian, but I don't know how terribly important it is to them. I think the church needs to focus on the Christian part of the equation.

Greg Devejian, *Albuquerque, New Mexico*

The Armenian-American Paradox

I didn't choose to be born in the United States, but I thank God that the United States opened its gates to Armenians after the Genocide and that we were able to come here. When I was growing up in the 1960s, a lot of the kids I hung out with belonged to the Armenian Youth Federation. At that time, the popular chant was for a free and independent Armenia. Many of my friends were often heard saying, "When Armenia is free, I'm going to move there."

Since independence in 1992, how many people have uprooted their families and moved to Armenia? You can count the number of people who have done that on one hand. In fact, rather than a mass repatriation of Armenia from the Diaspora, there's been a mass exodus of people from Armenia to the United States. Today, when I see those same kids who are now adults, I ask them, "You always said that you were waiting for this moment in history to go live in Armenia. Why don't you go?"

They don't go because people love America. The United States is our country and it is a wonderful country. That doesn't mean we have to lose our ethnicity, but "being Armenian" takes on a different dimension when we accept the United States as our home. We become American Armenians. Nobody has a problem with the Bolsetzis (Armenians from Istanbul, Turkey) having their own subculture or the Beirutzis (Armenians from Beirut, Lebanon) having their own subculture, or the Bakutzis or the Haiastanzis. But when it comes to American Armenians, there's a fear, or a stigma, that says we cannot have our own way of being Armenian.

In the early 1990s, when the Baku refugees began arriving in great numbers, nobody had a problem with putting Russian into the church. The church began translating everything into Russian to help those lost Armenians from Baku who didn't speak much, if any, Armenian. Well, what about English? There is a stigma about using English in the church that I don't understand.

It's time to decide if we are Armenians living in the United States who plan one day to leave and go back to our native homeland or if we are here to stay. If we are Armenians living here and we plan to stay here, then we not only should but must express our unique American-Armenian culture. Our subculture should influence all the aspects of our lives, including the church.

It is our Christian faith, not our Armenian language, that has sustained us through the centuries. If we place our faith second to our language, we will be the perpetrators of the next genocide—a genocide that will be far more devastating than the previous one.

If American Armenians chose to worship in the English language, let them.

People need to realize that we are all in the same boat. We are all attempting to become Christians. None of us is a Christian yet. We aspire to Christianity. We aspire to living Christian lives. It's a journey that we're all on together no matter what language you use to express it.

Reverend Father Krikor Sabounjian, *Holliston, Massachusetts*

INSIGHTS ON A COLLEGE DATE

When I was an undergraduate at Harvard, I dated a very American, non-Armenian girl. One night, I invited her to an Armenian Church Youth Organization dance. At the dance, I introduced her to my friends. She loved the people and the Armenian music. We had a great time, and we danced all night, but afterwards, on our walk home, she started to cry. I thought to myself, "Oh, no. What did I do?"

Then she surprised me by asking me if I knew how lucky I was to belong to a community of people. "You are part of something greater than yourself," she said. "I don't have anything like that in my life. Do you really know how lucky you are?"

I think I do, but it was very powerful to hear someone else say that.

James Kalustian, *Arlington, Massachusetts*

Study and Workshop Guide

The stories in *Descendants of Noah* were given in response to specific faith and heritage questions. Both the questions and response readings are listed below.

Use this index as a guide for study and discussion or to solicit storytelling from participants in a workshop. Feel free to replace references to the "Armenian Christian heritage" with your faith, denomination, or ethnic background in order to make the prompt questions your own.

Faith

A. Faith and daily life:
How does your living faith affect the decisions you have made in your life and/or make in your daily life?
What do you do that you may like to share with others that helps you keep your faith alive everyday? How might what you do be an example for others to help them become more alive in their faith?

Readings: 17, 32, 38, 50, 52, 53, 56, 57, 59, 60, 65, 66, 67, 73, 75, 107

B. Tested faith:
Can you recount one time or give one example of when your faith was tested and you persevered?
Have you ever, for a time, lost your faith? If so, when, how, why? Did you find your faith again? If so, how? If not, why not? Are you still searching?

Readings: 19, 21, 24, 27, 29, 35, 36, 39, 41, 42, 44, 52, 53, 55, 63, 72, 75, 86

C. Witnessed faith:
Sometimes seeing someone else's faith is easier than seeing your own. Can you share a story of witnessing another person's faith and tell us the lesson you learned?

Readings: 39, 40, 47, 48, 51, 54, 62, 69, 74, 79, 80

D. What does "living faith" mean to you?

Readings: 22, 25, 26, 34, 78

HERITAGE

A. Heritage or choice:
What, if anything, or who has contributed to your continued loyalty to the Armenian Christian heritage?
Why have you maintained your faith in the Armenian Christian heritage?
Have you explored other faiths, or churches, in your spiritual search and come back to the Armenian Church? If so, share your experience and learning. If you have not returned, why not?

Readings: 84, 93, 101, 104, 105, 108, 118, 126, 128, 133, 153, 155, 156, 159, 161, 162

B. Service and its rewards:
Has your involvement with the Armenian Christian community (church, clergy, volunteer, etc.) had a profound effect on you, your family and your life? If so, please give a specific example.
Can you give an example of one time when your involvement or service in the Armenian Christian community really made a difference? If you are active in any service, such as teaching Sunday school, why are you active? What is your motivation? If you are a member of the clergy, why did you choose this vocation?

Readings: 83, 102, 113, 119, 121, 129, 130, 132, 134, 135, 138, 139, 144, 145, 146, 147

C. Armenian Christianity and the world:
How, in your opinion, does the Armenian Christian heritage relate or fit with the world? What significant role has it played in your life, especially as you interact with other communities, nations, and the world?

Readings: 81, 83, 91, 93, 98, 99, 115, 137, 140, 145, 148, 150, 151, 152, 164, 165, 166, 168

D. Armenian Christianity and survival:

In 2001, the Armenian Apostolic Church celebrated 1700 years of Christianity. Do you think the Armenian Church will continue to survive? If so, how? Why?

What role does the Armenian Church serve today? How do you envision that role changing or remaining the same in the future?

Does the Armenian Church have to adapt for the future? What roadblocks does it face?

Readings: 94, 123, 125, 161, 163, 166, 167

Thematic Index

Abortion 29
Acceptance 27, 79
Adoption 76
Advice 29, 83
Aging 25, 51
Alzheimer's 25
Anger 36, 55, 119
Arguments 105, 166
Armenia 50, 79, 80, 91, 94, 107, 115, 120, 130, 138
Armenian Church
 In America 101, 102, 108, 113
 National Church 148
Appreciation 62, 133
Assimilation 123, 126, 127, 166, 167
Belief 22, 36, 78
Cancer 40, 41, 52
Change 67, 86
Character 56
Children 85, 118, 130, 132
Children, loss of 29, 35, 41, 53, 72
Choices 73, 84, 155, 156, 159, 161
Christianity
 Catholic 44, 148, 159
 Orthodox 57, 91, 94, 148, 150, 151, 156, 160
 Protestant 47, 113, 116, 148, 151, 156, 160
Clergy 24, 38, 44, 94, 119, 120, 127, 144
Comfort 161
Compassion 86
Connectedness 168
Culture 123, 125, 127, 128, 137
Daily life 22, 34, 38, 56, 73, 75, 81, 107, 128
Death 27, 29, 39, 40, 41, 53, 65, 72, 135
Decisions 22, 29

Diversity 123, 125, 127
Divine liturgy (*Badarak*) 108, 116
Divorce 36, 84
Doubt 27, 36
Dreams 58, 67
Empathy 91
Evangelization 91, 148
Fasting 112
Father 34, 39, 72, 101
Fear 39
Food 128, 134, 135, 136, 137
Forgiveness 35, 59, 164
Genocide 39, 54, 62, 86, 93, 99, 101, 164, 165, 166
Gifts 27, 42
God's plan 17, 32, 55, 58, 59, 60, 61, 63, 66, 102, 121
Grace 19, 99
Gratitude 39
Grief 35, 59
Healing 53, 74
Honesty 56
Hope 51, 52, 53
Human rights 86, 91
Humility 34
Identity 115, 123, 125, 127
Inspiration 22
Interdependence 160
Joy 47
Kindness 26, 42, 50, 62
Language, Armenian 98, 99, 108, 115, 162, 167
Leadership 105, 120
Learning 52, 57, 118
Letting go 34, 35, 38, 94
Listening 22, 38, 52, 83
Loss, of faith 36, 41, 58, 63
Love 25
Marriage 38, 66

Martyrdom 93
Meditation 34
Money 145, 146
Mother 25, 54
Obstacles 27
Openness 38
Outreach 42, 52, 83, 86, 91, 108, 136, 137, 138, 139, 140
Parents 69, 72, 107
Parishes 108, 113, 127, 137
Patience 55
Peace 75, 91
Perspective 17, 41
Preparedness 72, 75
Prayer 27, 34, 65, 70, 162
Pride 81
Priorities 67
Prodigal Son 35, 159
Protection 67
Resurrection 22, 24
Responsibility 72, 86, 91, 152
Sacraments 116, 160
Second chance 19
Scripture, Holy 21, 22, 52, 59
Service 105, 129, 130, 134, 135, 136, 147
Sex 22
Special days
  Lent 112
  Holy Thursday 74
  Armenian Genocide 166
Spiritual journey 22, 36, 44, 121, 156
Spiritual strength 38, 86
Stewardship 93, 94, 105
Sunday school 19, 25, 85, 132, 133
Survival 93, 115
Teaching 25, 85, 91, 132, 133
Tested faith 36, 41, 52, 53, 58, 59, 63, 75, 84, 86
Tradition 153, 161, 162, 163
Unity 104, 105
Witnessed faith 48, 80
Worship 80, 94, 119

Index of Storytellers

Anonymous, Fresno, California 147
Yeretzgin Sirarpi Feredjian Aivazian, Fresno, California 150
Marietta Arzumanyan, Belmont, Massachusetts 27
Julie Ashekian, Kensington, Connecticut 107, 130, 151
Carl Bazarian, Amelia Island, Florida 152
Oghda Boghosian, Fowler, California 99
Lauren Chalekian, Racine, Wisconsin 75, 85, 126, 132
†Reverend Father Haroutiun Dagley, South Euclid, Ohio 22, 24, 34, 38, 47, 94, 116
Jason Demerjian, Waltham, Massachusetts 38, 79, 159
Haig Deranian, Belmont, Massachusetts 19, 166
Greg Devejian, Albuquerque, New Mexico 113, 166
Yeretzgin Mariam Dingilian, Irvine, California 125
Reverend Father Stepanos Dingilian, Ph.D., Irvine, California 127
†Carla Donobedian, Fresno, California 52, 119
Reverend Father Stepanos Doudoukjian, Latham, New York 42, 140
Karen Durgarian, Hopkinton, Massachusetts 137
Karnig Durgarian, Hopkinton, Massachusetts 164
Lorraine Esraelian, Fowler, California 41
Marge Esraelian, Selma, California 41
Sarkis Gennetian, Watertown, Massachusetts 98
Geraldine Simonian Hagopian, Visalia, California 101
Richard Hagopian, Visalia, California 39, 93
Michael Haratunian, Glen Head, New York 105
Edgar Housepian, M.D., New York, New York 161
Lynn Jamie, Old Brookville, New York 25
Reverend Deacon Aren Jebejian, Chicago, Illinois 60
Ara Jeknavorian, Chelmsford, Massachusetts 26, 73, 132, 163
Deacon Allan Y. Jendian, Fresno, California 118, 129, 145
Matthew Ari Jendian, Ph.D., Clovis, California 123
George Kadamian, Racine, Wisconsin 74
Heidi Kadamian, Racine, Wisconsin 74
Yeretzgin Lana Kaishian, Yettem, California 32
Paulette Kalebjian, Fresno, California 155
The Reverend Louise Kalemkerian, Stamford, Connecticut 156
James Kalustian, Arlington, Massachusetts 56, 168
Deacon Patrick Kaprelian, Ridgewood, New Jersey 21
Oshyn Kasparian, Los Angeles, California 102
Reverend Father Vartan Kasparian, Visalia, California 69, 144

Virginia Kasparian, Selma, California 119
Siran Kassabian, Watertown, Massachusetts 112
Nick Kazarian, Fresno, California 160
Talene Kelegian, Racine, Wisconsin 139
Reverend Father Yeprem Kelegian, Racine, Wisconsin 51, 93, 128
Cecil Keshishian, Los Angeles, California 17
Judy Krikorian, Clovis, California 58
Very Reverend Father Krikor Maksoudian, Arlington, Massachusetts 53
Alice Ashchian-Martin, Watertown, Massachusetts 57
Michael Martin, Fowler, California 72
Virgine Kezarjian Mazmanian, Arlington, Massachusetts 62, 134, 165
Richard Melikian, Phoenix, Arizona 86
Sub-Deacon Francis K. Merzigian, New York, New York 44
Linda Miles, Fresno, California 76
Tom Miles, Fresno, California 42
Deacon Mitchell Mouradjian, New Rochelle, New York 55
Rachel Onanian Nadjarian, Ann Arbor, Michigan 39
Laurie Nalbandian, Fowler, California 63
Talin Nalbandian, Troy, New York 29
Seta Nersessian, Westwood, Massachusetts 80
Dr. Dennis R. Papazian, Troy, Michigan 129, 153, 161
Pat Paragamian, Racine, Wisconsin 34, 135
Perry Paragamian, Racine, Wisconsin 61
Marilyn L. Pattigan, Parlier, California 67, 104
Shant Petrossian, New York, New York 48, 115, 120
Paul Pogharian, Watertown, Massachusetts 36
Reverend Father Krikor Sabounjian, Holliston, Massachusetts 108, 167
Rose Samoulian, Sanger, California 136
Tom Samuelian, Yerevan, Armenia 50, 91
Merle Santerian, Huntingdon Valley, Pennsylvania 145
Martha Saraydarian, Englewood Cliffs, New Jersey 138
Irene Sarkisian, Woburn, Massachusetts 133
Yeghisabed Sarkisian, Fowler, California 59
Vi Selvian, Fresno, California 53
Gloria Semonian, Royal Oak, Michigan 35, 54, 70, 84
Charlie Shooshan, Newington, Connecticut 75, 81, 146
Sandy Soulakian, Chicago, Illinois 121
Mary Stevoff, Chicago, Illinois 40, 83, 128
Christopher Zakian, New York, New York 66, 78, 148, 162
Rose Zinakorjian, Chicago, Illinois 65, 101

A native of New England, Barbara Ghazarian is passionate about her Armenian heritage. Barbara lectures from coast to coast on Armenian-related topics to both Armenian and American audiences. She has years of experience teaching writing to continuing education adults in greater Boston. Her cookbook, *Simply Armenian: Naturally Healthy Ethnic Cooking Made Easy*, won Honorable Mention in the Writer's Digest 12th International Self-Published Book Awards. Today she splits her time between Monterey, California and Newport, Rhode Island, and is working on a novel also inspired by her ancestry.

Barbara may be reached at:
Mayreni Publishing
PO Box 5881
Monterey, CA 93944-5881

Or send her an e-mail at info2@mayreni.com
Visit her website at www.mayreni.com